Advance Praise for

Arrest Decisions: WHAT WORKS FOR THE OFFICER?

"In this ground-breaking study, Edith Linn, a former New York Police Department lieutenant, takes on the personal dimensions of arrest decisions. Some officers, suffering from low pay and high living costs, arrest for overtime and use a variety of techniques to maximize it. Others are deterred from arrest-making by the muddle of paperwork and the likelihood that a collar will interfere with childcare, second jobs, or family functions. Such officers may pass off their arrests to others, ignore criminal behavior, or try for a desk job. Overall, this exceptional work not only humanizes these officers but adds tremendously to our store of knowledge of policing and the factors that affect officers' behavior."

Martin D. Schwartz, Professor of Sociology, Ohio Presidential Research Scholar,
Ohio University

"Edith Linn's book *Arrest Decisions* is a fascinating, well-researched study of adaptive arrest behavior among New York City Police Department officers. Linn, a former NYPD lieutenant, proves that lengthy arrest procedures generate powerful private motives to make or avoid an arrest, and that officers control their arrest-making in furtherance of their own self-interest. Buttressing her analysis are the many participants' comments, which detail the problems in their daily lives and their frustration with the system. Linn's groundbreaking work is an outstanding contribution to the literature of policing and criminal justice. I would recommend it for any interested professor, researcher, student, and the average citizen."

John S. Dempsey, Captain, New York City Police Department (Ret.);
Professor Emeritus in Criminal Justice, State University of New York (SUNY)-
Schenectady County Community College;
Mentor in Criminal Justice and Public Administration, SUNY-Empire State College

"Anyone interested in exploring the full range of factors that enter a police officer's mind as he/she decides when and how often to arrest individuals should hurry up and read Edith Linn's *Arrest Decisions*. Linn brings these considerations to life through rigorous social science analysis buttressed with illuminating revelations of officers' confidential opinions. She uncloaks the determinants of this 'adaptive arrest behavior' as she astutely combines the practical experience of a former police lieutenant and the analytical skills of a sociologist.

The book examines the intersection of the arresting process with organizational, situational, and personal factors, but it is in the area of personal factors that Linn breaks new ground. She examines such factors as post-work commitments, the burdens of the arrest process, attitudes towards arrest, personal concerns, personal finances, and pre-incident proclivity to make or decline arrests.

This volume is an important contribution to the literature on police behavior and other scholars will be well advised to replicate this valuable study. I highly recommend this work."

Eli B. Silverman, Professor Emeritus, John Jay College of Criminal Justice;
Author, NYPD Battles Crime: Innovative Strategies in Policing

Arrest Decisions

NEW PERSPECTIVES
IN CRIMINOLOGY
AND CRIMINAL JUSTICE

Jeffrey Ian Ross
General Editor

Vol. 5

PETER LANG
New York • Washington, D.C./Baltimore • Bern
Frankfurt am Main • Berlin • Brussels • Vienna • Oxford

EDITH LINN

Arrest Decisions

WHAT WORKS FOR THE OFFICER?

PETER LANG
New York • Washington, D.C./Baltimore • Bern
Frankfurt am Main • Berlin • Brussels • Vienna • Oxford

Library of Congress Cataloging-in-Publication Data

Linn, Edith.
Arrest decisions: what works for the officer? / Edith Linn.
p. cm. — (New perspectives in criminology and criminal justice; v. 5)
Includes bibliographical references and index.
1. Police—New York (State)—New York. 2. Arrest—New York (State)—
New York. 3. Criminal procedure—New York (State)—New York.
4. New York (N.Y.). Police Dept. I. Title.
HV8148.N52L55   363.2'32—dc22   2008042747
ISBN 978-1-4331-0058-1
ISSN 1555-3418

Bibliographic information published by **Die Deutsche Bibliothek**.
Die Deutsche Bibliothek lists this publication in the "Deutsche
Nationalbibliografie"; detailed bibliographic data is available
on the Internet at http://dnb.ddb.de/.

Cover design by Clear Point Designs

The paper in this book meets the guidelines for permanence and durability
of the Committee on Production Guidelines for Book Longevity
of the Council of Library Resources.

© 2009 Peter Lang Publishing, Inc., New York
29 Broadway, 18th floor, New York, NY 10006
www.peterlang.com

Printed in the United States of America

People do not exist just for organizations.
They track in all kinds of mud from the rest of their lives.
—Charles Perrow

CONTENTS

TABLES

FIGURES

SERIES EDITOR'S PREFACE

The municipal police garner considerable mass media and academic attention. Issues such as patrol, response time, corruption, and violence frequently become primary subjects for mass media and scholarly inquiry and result in numerous classic studies, seminal pieces of research, and at least half a dozen English language peer-reviewed journals. Admittedly, the general public has a considerable amount of "common sense" knowledge regarding the law enforcement profession; however, public opinion is also heavily tainted by several misconceptions. The reality is that the practice and craft of policing is more complicated than meets the untrained eye. Few people, including scholars, are willing to take the time to notice, analyze, and comprehend the nuances of police behavior. Collecting accurate and reliable information on police conduct and interpreting it in a meaningful fashion is not a simple task.

As the editor of Peter Lang's series "New Perspectives in Criminology and Criminal Justice," I'm excited to introduce you to Edith Linn's well-researched book *Arrest Decisions: What Works for the Officer?*. The fifth installment in Lang's series, this is a formidable piece of cutting-edge scholarship that pushes the boundaries of police science as well as the disciplines of criminology and criminal justice.

Linn, a former New York City police lieutenant and now a professor of criminal justice, analyzes the decision-making process behind typical police actions in arrest situations. The majority of research that precedes Linn's work has examined the factors embedded in the immediate incident—particularly the suspect's behavior. Few of these past inquiries have looked at the personal concerns of police officers themselves in weighing whether to take an individual into custody. Using both qualitative and quantitative research, Linn emphasizes these overlooked and nontraditional kinds of factors involving the decisions police officers make in arrest situations. Linn documents not only these decisions, but also the context in which they are made—including contributing factors such as an individual's possible overtime needs, private commitments, and aversion to the arrest process itself.

I'm sure that scholars, instructors, practitioners, and students in policing/law enforcement will be intrigued by Linn's book.

Jeffrey Ian Ross, Ph.D.

WHY THIS BOOK?

Arrest processing may seem too mundane a topic to warrant the attention of researchers, especially compared to the immediate factors officers face when making arrest decisions. Yet what an officer experiences *after* putting on handcuffs can profoundly influence whether that arrest is made in the first place.

In the New York City Police Department, where I spent 21 years, arrest processing takes about ten hours. The length, difficulties, and risks of these procedures affect the personal lives of officers, and they respond by adapting their arrest-making behavior to their individual needs. Sometimes they pursue "collars for dollars," but more often they put their efforts into avoiding arrest. As a result, justice and public safety are compromised, financial resources are wasted, and officer morale is depleted.

With over 37,000 officers, the NYPD is by far the largest police agency in America. Its world renown and prominence in law enforcement scholarship would in themselves make this issue extremely important. Yet the adverse effects of arrest processing delays also have been reported in agencies as diverse as the Metropolitan Police in London and the 11-officer department in Melissa, Texas. Hopefully this book will lead other scholars and practitioners to address these problems.

ORGANIZATION AND STYLE

The largest portion of the book (Chapters 3 through 12) examines the survey responses of 506 police officers who regularly patrol the streets of New York. They are asked about their patrol style, pre-arrest planning, finances, post-work commitments, arrest processing aversions, arrest-control tactics, arrest-related attitudes, overall arrest determinants, and attempts by management to control their arrest behavior. Within the chapters are findings for the sample as a whole, and for subgroups such as high-arrest and low-arrest officers, males and females, midnight, day, and evening tours, and high-crime and low-crime boroughs. Appendix A summarizes the findings by group and subgroups rather than by chapter, to provide an alternative perspective. The survey itself is reproduced in Appendix B. The final chapter suggests ways to improve arrest processing and minimize its many negative effects. It discusses arrest processing in other large cities, as revealed in a second survey, found in Appendix C.

One challenge in presenting my findings is the jargon used by the NYPD. Slang, acronyms, and other specialized terms are defined when first used in the text, and also explained in the Glossary. Participants' comments are presented verbatim, despite their occasional use of profanity, in order to preserve their emotional content.

ACKNOWLEDGMENTS

Many individuals were generous in their help for this project. Drs. Ned Benton, Jennifer Groscup, and Barry Spunt of John Jay College are the first to come to mind. Dr. Linda Nagel moonlighted as my first editor. Dr. David Klinger freely shared his considerable expertise.

Money always helps. A grant from the National Science Foundation (#0136630/01) enabled me to delegate data input to my dedicated colleague, Lisa Williams, and to bribe survey participants with coffee, bagels, and other treats.

The New York City Police Department's assistance was more complicated. Had the NYPD not given me a career, and allowed me to survey over 600 officers on company time, there would be no book. On the other hand, once I had left the department, my formal request for updated information about arrest processing was met with great resistance. As a high-ranking police colleague confided to me, "They just don't want you to have this information." Ultimately, a surreptitious end-run around the department enabled me to learn that arrest processing had gotten even *longer* than it was at the time of the original study.

The most inspiring help came from the participants in the two surveys. Heartfelt thanks go to my fellow officers, whose responses and passionate comments reveal the human cost of a foolish system. And sincere gratitude also goes to police supervisors from across the country, whose detailed accounts of their own agencies' procedures prove that there *are* better ways to process arrests.

CHAPTER ONE

Adaptive Arrest Behavior
An Open Secret

Our culture has long had a fascination with police officers. Their armed presence evokes a strange mix of comfort and fear. Their actions on behalf of "the State" are layered with meaning and fraught with controversy. Their persona is inflated by ballads, books, melodramas, news accounts, and their own media-savvy agencies. Whether we view them as heroes, rogues, buffoons, or tormented souls, police officers are always worthy of our attention—never "just like everybody else."

Researchers who try to explain officer behavior have been no less affected by this police mystique. When writing about *why* officers make arrests, they dwell upon motives that seem unique or "subcultural" (e.g., Skolnick, 1966; Niederhoffer, 1967; Westley, 1970; Kappeler, Sluder, & Alpert, 1994), while disregarding personal incentives that might be common to *any* worker. They highlight distinctive sociological, psychological, and organizational elements of the arrest decision (e.g., Bittner, 1970; Black, 1971; Riksheim & Chermak, 1993; Novak et al., 2002; Chappell et al., 2006) while ignoring mundane factors like overtime and arduous arrest procedures—that is, the personal benefits and burdens of arrest-making itself.

Yet the *process* of arrest-making, with its personal consequences for the officer, may be one of the most critical arrest determinants of all. Consider the 37,000-member New York City Police Department, which may have the longest and most stressful arrest processing in America. These procedures generate powerful private motives to either make or avoid an arrest at any given time. The most common personal arrest benefit is overtime, calculated at time-and-a-half rates, taken in cash or compensatory time. The personal costs of arrest processing are its intrusion upon officers' off-duty time, and its multiple risks such as disciplinary action and combative arrestees. Thus, controlling the occurrence and timing of an arrest is *adaptive*—that is, it is a way for officers to improve their incomes, personal schedules, and working conditions.

ARREST PROCESSING IN THE NYPD

I was able to examine the effects of protracted arrest processing as a 21-year member of the NYPD, and then as a researcher in 2002. At that time, the average arrest took 9.57 hours to complete, and cost $174.68 in over-time (Criminal Justice Bureau, 2001). In 2007, average city-wide process-ing time had increased to *10.45* hours (Criminal Justice Bureau, 2007) despite an "upgraded" computer system installed four years earlier.

Police management would defend the current methods as a vast im-provement over decades past, when processing could last for two to three *days.* (Indeed, retired officers reminisce about storing a bed roll and shav-ing kit at Central Booking to use when they brought in a collar.) Officials might also claim that New York's successful crime-fighting strategies re-quire a high number of arrests, which inevitably overburdens the process-ing system. But this cannot explain why, long after the "Zero-Tolerance" policies of the 1990s were instituted, police executives, borough district attorneys, and court administrators have yet to accommodate these in-creased arrests. Neither can volume explain why, within the five New York City boroughs, arrest quantity seems to have no relationship to processing times (see Table 1-1). Rather, the causes are embedded within the jerry-built processing system—a system hobbled by redundant paperwork, mis-used personnel, broken equipment, backward technology, dispersed facili-ties, and conflicts among police units and justice agencies.

Nearly 95% of adult arrests made in New York are "on-line" cases, that is, prisoners held in police custody for about 22 hours awaiting arraign-ment before a judge. The rest are mostly Desk Appearance Ticket (DAT) cases, wherein select low-level offenders are issued a future court date and then released on their own recognizance. Under typical conditions, uni-formed members of the service (UMOS) take the arrestee to the station house in the precinct where the offense occurred. Officers report to the Desk Supervisor, who logs in the prisoner's identifying information, per-sonal property and/or evidence confiscated, and physical condition.

A person arrested for driving while intoxicated (DWI) will then be brought to a blood-alcohol testing facility, a step that can easily add two hours to arrest processing times. Even longer delays can ensue when the prisoner needs to go to the hospital for medical treatment or psychiatric evaluation—a common situation, because so many indigent arrestees are either ill, injured, or addicted. Even prisoners who legitimately possess prescription medications must relinquish them (as they may be fraudu-lently labeled) and get a fresh supply through the hospital emergency room. So protracted are these ER visits that officers sometimes counsel their prisoners to not disclose their medical problems to Central Book-ing's medical screening personnel.

Eventually the arresting officer fills out an On-line Booking Sheet and Precinct Complaint Report (a "61"), each of which requires over 100 entries. Much of the basic arrest information—officer, perpetrator, victim, time and place of occurrence, and so forth—is then written on additional forms such as a Property Voucher, Supporting Deposition, Medical Treatment of Prisoner, Stop and Frisk Report, Request for Lab Analysis, and Aided Card (recording assistance rendered to non-prisoners). Lest some form be forgotten, officers may also prepare an Arrest Documentation Checklist (the "Form Form").

At the time of the study, the majority of officers could not input their own arrest data into the On-Line Booking System. OLBS, designed in the 1970s, was so idiosyncratic that only very regular users knew all its "tricks." The computer system lacked the most basic word-processing features, and many entries could not be changed without re-typing entire sections. "Error" messages regularly flashed on screen without offering a clue as to what was wrong. Thus, to input the reports and obtain computer-generated serial numbers, the typical officer had to find a staff member who was willing and able to assist. This could be a civilian police administrative aid (PAA) or a uniformed arrest processing officer (APO) assigned in-house to help struggling colleagues.

In 2003, OLBS was replaced with the Omniform System. Now, with little assistance, officers can type, correct, print, and get serial numbers for their on-screen Arrest Reports and Complaint Reports. But the new Omniform System fails to include many of the most common arrest forms, and it cannot transfer data from one on-screen document to another, so they must be retyped over and over. Worse, the Department still requires that many forms, including those in the Omniform System, first be handwritten (unless it's a Property Voucher, which must be hand-written and then *typed on a typewriter*). Thus, the help a PAA or APO is still frequently needed.

Once arresting officers have their serial numbers, they are ready to electronically fingerprint and photograph the prisoner. Paperwork has to be completed within about three hours, and then sent to the District Attorney's Intake Office, either by erratic fax machine or hand-delivery. (Even the Omniform System documents cannot be transferred electronically to the DA's Office, but must be printed out and faxed individually.) Officers then confer with an Assistant District Attorney (ADA) or a surrogate officer-deponent, who draws up the primary arraignment document, the Complaint Affidavit.

With on-line cases, police employees track each of six processing stages in the On-Line-Prisoner Arraignment System. OLPA was created to locate specific prisoners and processing delays (inevitable in so convoluted a system), and has become yet another management tool to determine or deflect blame. And while OLPA helps keep detainees from getting "lost in the system," its logging procedures add to the length and expense of processing.

Though the NYPD's Criminal Justice Bureau oversees arrest processing citywide, each borough prepares complaint affidavits through its own procedures established by its district attorney and administrative judge. Their offices set policies regarding whether to impose additional arrest forms, whether officers will be interviewed in person, by video, by phone, or by interactive computer, and who among the arresting officers, ADAs, or officer-proxies will operate the complaint-writing software. These offices also control how many Intake ADAs and arraignment judges will be working, and until what hour. Such decisions, combined with differences in staffing, equipment, and prisoner volume, created inter-borough disparities in arrest-processing speed and difficulty. At the extremes, the mean arrest-to-complaint-sworn time (when the arresting officer has completed the final arrest processing task) was 8.10 hours in Queens, but 11.35 hours in Staten Island (Criminal Justice Bureau, 2001) just before the study. Queens processing was thus nearly three and a half hours shorter, though it processed almost six times as many arrests as Staten Island. An overview of on-line arrest volume and arrest-to-complaint-sworn times is as follows:

Table 1-1. *On-line Arrests and Average Arrest-to-Complaint-Sworn Times in Each Borough and Citywide in 2001*

Borough	# of On-line Arrests	Arrest-to-Complaint-Sworn Time
Manhattan	91,393	10.48 hrs.
Brooklyn	82,300	8.28 hrs.
Bronx	50,082	10.68 hrs.
Queens	49,527	8.10 hrs.
Staten Island	8,406	11.35 hrs
Citywide	289,708	9.57 hrs.

To further complicate matters, these arrest-processing policies have a different impact depending on the tour. Arresting officers on the 4-to-12 shift who do not finish their paperwork before the DA's Intake Office closes for the night will be rescheduled to finish processing on the day tour. Most officers dislike being rescheduled, because it disrupts their sleep patterns and personal schedules while affording no overtime. But if officers make an arrest just before their regular day off (RDO), and must be rescheduled to work on that day, they are paid a sizable amount of overtime. And, if the officers have plans for the following evening, being rescheduled can jibe perfectly. So we find, for instance, that every Saturday night before the annual Super Bowl, there was an increase in arrests and subsequent reschedules, allowing the arresting officers to finish processing well before Sunday's big game.

In contrast to those on the 4-to-12 shift, officers on the midnight shift end their tour as the DA's Intake Office opens and are never rescheduled. Thus their arrests have the highest potential for overtime, making the tour attractive to "heavy hitters" who make many arrests. Presently, many officers seem to choose the midnight tour because, aside from paying ten percent higher salaries, it allows them to work a day job or to get their children off to school in the morning.

ADAPTING TO THE SYSTEM

From their first stationhouse roll call, New York City patrol officers begin to absorb the skills and rationales to control their arrest-making. Here, many officers speak freely of their need for arrest overtime to pay for a car, a vacation, or their children's braces. One discusses a desire for arrest "comp time" to make up for days deducted as punishment. Another vows to arrest "any dirtbag that comes along" to get off his foot post. Some officers mention that they were up all night with a hot date or a sick baby and are thus in no condition to stay late with an arrest. Others talk about a class, a second job, or a party after work that would preclude their making an arrest. One officer, itching from contact with a lice-infested prisoner, declares that he will never again arrest a derelict. Those car-pooling together coordinate their arrest plans to accommodate their transportation needs going home. Officers poll one another as to who that day would offer or take an unwanted arrest.

When these arrest-sharing arrangements fall neatly into place, they have little impact on arrest decisions. But sometimes officers who have arranged to pass off their arrest find the "catchers" tied up with other patrol incidents. Occasionally, those officers most willing to take arrests are "capped out," forbidden by management to make any more cash overtime. On Super Bowl Sunday or on holidays, officers may not find a single colleague willing to take their arrest. At other periods, like the pre-Christmas shopping season, nearly every officer is out scrambling for arrest overtime. Thus, peer cooperation cannot guarantee that on a given day an officer will be able to make or avoid an arrest.

Some officers therefore feel a need to modify their patrol style to enhance their "arrest control." On an arrest-avoiding day, they may keep themselves busy with summonses and service calls, drive slowly and noisily to crimes in progress, shun blocks where arrests "fall into your lap," and forego proactive measures such as license plate checks and stop-and-frisks. They may avoid the types of people and the kinds of arguments that get them "pissed off." They may construe incidents as non-crimes, or ignore them entirely And on an arrest-seeking day, they may do exactly the opposite—rush to incidents, initiate interventions, provoke disputants, and pat down "known criminals"—particularly late in the tour, when arrests mean maximized overtime.

Oft-repeated maxims endorse officer self-interest as a rationale for adaptive arrest behavior. "Your job is to get home safe at the end of eight hours" and "Your family comes first" remind fellow officers not to be too self-sacrificing. "Make the Job work for you" celebrates the officer's ability to control the timing and type of arrest, to garner perks usually reserved for non-patrol assignments—more money, timely sign-out, or less unpleasantness. Other expressions justify adaptive arrest behavior by alluding to the "revolving door" nature of arrests. The failure to arrest a suspect is rationalized with a comment like "He'll get locked up next time he does something," while an arrest made on shaky legal grounds is excused with "This makes up for all the things this guy's done that he never got caught for." Capturing the broad disillusionment with the entire "system" is the common refrain, "The Job's not on the level."

Supervisors struggle to keep officers content and arrests honest. They may occasionally indulge subordinates who ask for an arrest-prone or arrest-proof assignment and may give a disproportionate number of non-arrest posts to women officers with young children. They may ask officers "looking for a collar" to identify themselves for the benefit of those hoping not to get stuck. They may help negotiate arrest-processing responsibilities. They may assign a simple end-of-tour arrest to the next tour, if it can spare an extra officer. But even the most diligent sergeants are unable to oversee every potential arrest scene and would incur great resentment if they tried. Moreover, sergeants sometimes feel they must barter for the cooperation of subordinates, even if it means "hanging back" from problematic arrest situations or accepting questionable arrest decisions.

Commanding officers are less familiar than sergeants with their officers' individual motives. They must focus on the "heavy hitters" who run up department overtime and to a lesser extent, on the "empty suits" who "get paid for doing nothing"—an approach that often has perverse results. The most opportunistic officers may escape notice by balancing arrests and avoidance. The most conscientious crime-fighters may be denied scheduled overtime tours or reassigned to posts with few arrest opportunities. The least active officers may escape scrutiny by occasionally "picking up" a shoplifter or other ready-made arrest or by arresting a hapless violator who might ordinarily receive a summons.

STUDYING ADAPTIVE ARREST BEHAVIOR

These observations are at odds with the prevailing image of arrest discretion, wherein officers randomly respond to situations, discover an offense, and then weigh a host of incident-related factors like offense seriousness, suspect and victim traits, presence of witnesses and bystanders, and so forth (see, e.g., Riksheim & Chermak, 1993; National Academy of Sciences, 2004). In the above description, personal concerns *predisposed* officers to make or avoid arrest, affecting which situations they handle and how they handle them. But to what extent are such behaviors typical?

In 2002, 655 NYPD officers responded to a questionnaire about how personal considerations affect arrest-making. Do the officers try to maximize overtime by avoiding arrests until the end of their tour? Do they plan their patrol day with a specific arrest outcome in mind? Do financial pressures encourage more arrest-making? Do post-work commitments and aversive arrest procedures lead to fewer arrests? Which personal factors— those that favor arrest, or those that disfavor it—are more influential? What special tactics are used to facilitate or evade arrest-making? What attitudes do officers hold to rationalize this behavior? Do they give as much decisional weight to personal factors as to other known arrest variables? Are they swayed by management's efforts to curb such behavior? Finally, do the responses differ according to whether the participants are high-arrest or low-arrest officers, or male or female? Whether they work the low-visibility midnight shift or in daylight hours? Whether patrolling in a high-crime, slow-processing borough, or one with low crime and faster processing?

A second survey examines arrest processing in other large other police agencies. Do some have arduous procedures like the NYPD? Do others make processing quick and easy—and less likely to influence arrest decisions? If so, then how is this accomplished? Do such agencies have simpler procedures, more advanced technology, better-trained officers, different overtime policies, greater delegation of processing tasks, or some other feature that the NYPD could adopt?

But before examining the results of the two surveys, we will address a more immediate question: Why hasn't adaptive arrest behavior received more attention in the first place?

CHAPTER TWO

Research Linked to Adaptive Arrest Behavior

No research on police behavior has directly examined the seeking or avoidance of arrest in furtherance of personal interests At best, this phenomenon has appeared as a scholarly aside, to be noted but never probed. For instance, James Q. Wilson (1968:83-84) writes:

> The patrolman's decision whether and how to intervene in a situation depends on his evaluation of the costs and benefits of various kinds of action. Though the substantive criminal law seems to imply a mandate...in fact for most officers there are considerations of utility that equal or exceed in importance those of duty or morality, especially for the more common and less serious laws.

Wilson's observation is buried in his *Varieties of Police Behavior*, a work famous for its exploration of *department-wide* arrest tendencies. Similarly, in *The Ambivalent Force* (1985:171), Blumberg and Niederhoffer's collection of prominent writings on police, this pragmatic side of arrest decisions is noted only in a chapter introduction to the subject:

> Does each officer have to meet an arrest quota for that month? What time of day does an incident take place? Is it near the end of a shift or the beginning of a tour? Will the police officer have to spend hours after duty in processing an arrest? Will this interfere with a social or family engagement? Does the department pay overtime for additional hours of work? Does the officer need the additional compensation? *Although rarely taken into account, these seemingly prosaic factors loom as controlling and compelling determinants of action.* [italics added].

Yet there is an abundance of scholarship *indirectly* related to the phenomenon of adaptive arrest behavior. We will review writings on police ethics, organizational behavior, occupational personality, motivation, and arrest discretion and then examine research on the variables specifically addressed in the study. Finally, we will reflect on why adaptive arrest behavior has not been examined directly.

LABELING THE PHENOMENON

In looking at other writings on adaptive arrest behavior, we might first ask how it should be classified. Is it a manifestation of a police officer's broad discretion, long recognized by both researchers and practitioners? Is it a subtle form of corruption? Or, is it best understood as a normal employee reaction to peculiar organizational incentives?

Experts disagree as to how broadly to define police discretion Criminologist Jerome Skolnick (1966) recognized both *delegated* discretion, options explicitly granted by rules or statutes, and *unauthorized* discretion, options not explicitly granted. Similarly expansive is the legal scholar Kenneth Culp Davis (1969), for whom discretion meant any choice of action or inaction (presumably even an unfair one) made by officers, given the effective limits to their power. The legal philosopher Ronald Dworkin (1977) referred to discretion as the "hole in the donut," the freedom to act in situations not covered by existing laws or regulations. Ethicist John Kleinig (1996) argued that the term should refer to only legitimate options, that is, those consonant with normative professional standards.

Yet despite these varied definitions, writings on arrest discretion have not actually examined *all* of the officer's possible considerations but only those options informed by the officer's personal notion of "how to get the job done." Whether they are legitimate discretionary factors, like offense seriousness, or "illegitimate" ones, like class or gender, *they are rationalized by the officer as a proper way to do police work* In contrast, self-interested arrest concerns like overtime and post-work commitments are rationalized by a personal concept of the *proper way to live one's life*, that is, the best balance between conflicting duties and competing selves. Kleinig (1997:74) is rare among police observers in speaking of this dilemma:

> Does our chief loyalty lie to our partner, our department, the commissioner, our family, or to the professional standards that are implicit in the kind of work we do? These are not easy questions...and sometimes they will involve "defining decisions," in which we decide what sort of person we will be.

While the negative aspects of arrest discretion and self-interested arrest behavior are alike, the potential benefits differ. Discretion may compromise equal treatment, due process, and deterrence (Kleinig, 1996; Brooks, 1997); the same charges can be made regarding adaptive arrest behavior. But discretion, being rooted in a professional norm, can also serve some greater good, such as individualizing justice, preserving patrol resources, or being responsive to neighborhood priorities (Brooks, 1997). Self-interested arrest considerations, on the other hand, further no public interest. Whatever their benefits—personal safety, income, self-fulfillment, family cohesion, and so forth—they are confined to the private sphere of the officer.

If adaptive arrest-making is distinct in motive and outcome from arrest discretion, might it better be classified as a form of misconduct? It seemingly fits Lawrence Sherman's definition of police corruption, "the illegal use of organizational power for personal gain" (1978:30), especially if the self-interest blatantly overrides all normative considerations (e.g., arresting without probable cause to earn overtime, or releasing a felon to avoid arrest processing.) Moreover, in my observations, the behavior is "taught" to officers in the same way other professions convey deviant practices to their members, that is, by early and extensive exposure to specific means, motives, and rationalizations (Sutherland, 1949; Klockars, 1983).

The view that adaptive arrest behavior is corrupt must be tempered, however, by three considerations. First, the "personal gain" in adaptive arrest decisions may entail laudable objectives. Who can entirely fault officers for trying to add some overtime to their relatively meager paychecks (De La Cruz, 2000; Weiss, 2001) or see more of their children? Second, such personal benefits are rarely the entire motive, prompting a blatantly false arrest or dereliction of duty. Rather, the self-interest is weighed with other arrest factors of varying appropriateness. Third, unlike a bribe or gratuity, the personal gain in seeking or evading arrests is unavoidably attached to that arrest decision. That is, regardless of motive, *every* arrest promises both money and misery.

The most fruitful alternative may be to view adaptive arrest behavior as a "normal" response to organizational and personal imperatives. It is to that perspective that we now turn.

ADAPTIVE ARREST-MAKING AS ORGANIZATIONAL BEHAVIOR

Modern police departments are bureaucratic organizations (Fogelson, 1977; Brown, 1988; Wilson, 1989). Police officers may wield more power and attract more attention than other entry-level employees, but their relationship within their organization follows some familiar patterns.

Because bureaucratic organizations involve and regulate only a limited segment of their members' selves and roles, sociologists classify them as *secondary* or *segmental* groups. These are contrasted with *primary* groups, such as the family, which engage the sentiments and behaviors of members in almost all their selves and roles (Merton, 1957; Coser, 1956; Downs, 1967). Writings about the police organization typically portray it as a primary group, enveloping officers in its ethos. Yet my own observations of ordinary patrol officers suggest that for the majority of them, the police agency is decidedly a secondary group, not a primary one.

Organizations can only "partially include" the entire person (Allport, 1933). Yet, it is the entire person—an officer with a personal life—who comes to work. Philip Selznik (1948:26–27) wrote of this dilemma:

Individuals have a propensity to resist depersonalization, to spill over the boundaries of their segmentary roles, to participate as wholes. The formal systems...cannot take account of the deviations thus introduced and consequently break down as instruments of control when relied upon alone. The whole individual raises new problems for the organization, partly because of the needs of his own personality, partly because he brings with him a set of established habits as well, perhaps, as commitments to special groups outside the organization.

In his book, *Inside Bureaucracy*, Anthony Downs (1967) drew on these earlier theorists to develop several propositions concerning organizations that mirror my own observations of behavior within the NYPD. Downs began with the hypothesis that members of organizations are significantly motivated by their own self-interest, even when acting in a purely official capacity. Among possible actions, they chose those that resulted in the highest personal "utility rating." Downs noted two reasons why the private motive and social function of work can never mesh: First, the private motive serves the interests of workers themselves, while the social function serves the interests of others. Second, workers' roles outside their primary employment generate desires, attitudes, and behaviors that inevitably influence their actions in their role as employee. Thus, it is unlikely that an officer's need for overtime or family time will regularly coincide with the agency's need for overtime control or arrest productivity.

Downs anticipated the imperfect symbiosis of a few officers who make many arrests and the many officers who make few, as seen in the NYPD and other police agencies. He stated that in any organization with formal job descriptions, the particular abilities and personalities of the individuals assigned to each job will never mesh perfectly with the tasks they are supposed to carry out. As a result, tasks formally assigned to one person are in fact performed by one or more others.

The use of arrest-control tactics to advance personal objectives also has parallels in all organizations, according to Downs. Depending on whether assigned duties favor or oppose their own interests, subordinates will "zealously expedite some orders, carry out others with only mild enthusiasm, drag their feet seriously on still others, and completely ignore a few" (77–78). Where official regulations are ambiguous, officials will select the "proper" administrative rules to apply in specific situations.

Police officers are not alone in resisting supervisory incursions into their discretionary domain. Control of members in bureaucratic organizations is universally difficult, wrote Downs, and the greater the effort made to control subordinates, the greater will be their effort to evade or counteract such control. Like police sergeants, most first-line supervisors in organizations find they must bend rules in exchange for work output. And, like police commanders who focus on "heavy hitters" and "do-nothings," most civilian executives must focus on performance indicators that either significantly deviate from targeted standards, or attract negative feedback from external monitors. As a result, they overlook information about subordinates' performance that falls outside these criteria.

The negative effects of excessive paperwork and procedures are also common to organizations. In 1940, Robert Merton wrote of how the true goal of an organization often is displaced by the more immediate objective of faithfully adhering to procedure. Wilson (1989) similarly observed that in government bureaus the trappings of "productivity"—records, reports, statistical sheets, and so forth—substitute for truer but less tangible gauges of effectiveness.

Wilson (1989) has written extensively about worker disenchantment and self-serving behaviors. These problems are particularly acute in "coping organizations" like police departments, where outputs and outcomes are not readily observable. In such organizations, official goals (such as "educating children" or "arresting criminals") are too vague or ambitious to be useful. As a result, tasks come to be shaped by the incentives valued by the members. To add to the problem, executives in coping agencies need to cultivate those outside constituencies who influence their careers. When such groups complain, executives ostentatiously reassign responsibilities or replace "unsatisfactory" performers, thus appearing not to "back up" their subordinates. This is precisely what occurs when, after a controversial police incident, the top brass summarily assign the officers involved to unarmed desk duty and transfer their superiors to some career-ending outpost.

Another discouraging factor for workers is the constraints on raises and other incentives, according to Wilson. Individual members of public agencies cannot lawfully retain any surplus profits (e.g., police officers cannot keep a portion of the fines from their summonses). Moreover, such members find it difficult to define or demonstrate the attained objective for which a reward is merited (e.g., police officers cannot demand raises because of reduced crime rates). In addition, their accomplishments cannot be evaluated without making political, and therefore conflict-ridden, judgments (e.g., officers' aggressive crime-fighting tactics are as likely to draw a civilian complaint as a commendation). Faced with these constraints, public employees veer toward more personal objectives.

The belief that "politics" undermines a fair, standardized system of advancement reflects a cynicism common among police officers and other employees. Civil servants often suspect that management schemes to promote on "merit" are simply a covert way to advance the lucky few who have the patronage of a high official or outside "rabbi" (an expression not confined to the police). Merton (1957) wrote that workers in bureaucracies favor a standardized promotion method because it reduces in-group competition and bolsters *esprit de corps*. Such bureaucratic procedures attain a moral legitimacy, even a sanctification.

The foregoing organizational writings anticipate the self-interested arrest behavior of police officers. They show that many traits of police agencies are common in bureaucratic institutions, particularly those run by the government. And, more broadly, they suggest that police behavior could be better understood if we recognize the commonalities of officers and other working people. Many scholars have been reluctant to do this, as the next section shows.

OFFICER TRAITS AND THE "POLICE PERSONALITY"

Studies have found that individual officer characteristics, such as education, race, and gender, seem to have little effect on behavior (Riksheim & Chermak, 1993; Brooks, 1997; White, 2007) But a number of researchers have posited that the police experience creates a unique occupational personality and subculture with a shared rationale for arrest. Others suggested that certain major personality dimensions interact to create several officer "types," some more arrest-prone than others. These perspectives may contribute to our understanding of arrest behavior, but do not account for the wide variation among individual officers.

Among the literature offering a single prototype is Skolnick's (1966) description of the officer's "working personality." It is molded by danger and authority, and manifested in preemptive actions toward anyone whose appearance or demeanor matches that of a "symbolic assailant." Niederhoffer (1967) saw cynicism as the dominant mindset, eroding the officer's responsiveness to the wishes of both the citizenry and agency executives. Wilson (1968) contended that the officer's moral judgments of the victim and suspect form the basis of most arrest decisions. Bittner (1970) felt that the legitimized power to use physical coercion is the officer's defining trait, while Ericson (1982) stated that the officer's need to "reproduce order" determined whether and how to intervene.

Studies of police personality have been challenged for relying on small samples, impressionistic observations, and imprecise concepts (Lefkowitz, 1975; Herbert, 1998; Walker & Katz, 2008). Later research has questioned the existence of a widespread and distinct police subculture (Jermier, Slocum, Fry, & Gaines, 1991; Worden, 1995; Herbert, 1998; Paoline et al.,

2000, Cochran & Bromley, 2003). Perhaps the primary criticism is that the concept is increasingly out of date (National Academy of Sciences, 2004; Walker & Katz, 2008). As early as 1984, Bahn noted that the trend toward diversity among officers is inevitably leading to less in-group cohesion and more identification with civilian segments of society. There are now more racial and ethnic minorities, more women, and more gay officers, each claiming a distinct culture. With more shared parenting, male officers with working wives as well as female officers must make child-care duties a high priority. Older and college-educated recruits bring a wider world view. Police residency "sprawl," to suburbs ever more remote from the city, limits peer socializing to work hours. Steady tours encourage officers to develop their "off-duty" lives (Bahn, 1984; Martin, 1997). All these developments foster non-police identities and priorities that could influence on-duty actions.

Another approach to police personality is to classify officers into several personality types based on select dimensions that relate to arrest behavior. For instance, White (1972) classified officers by whether they attend to the immediate event or final outcome of a patrol situation, and whether they treat citizens as individuals or as stereotypes. Broderick (1977) grouped officers along the dimensions of commitment to constitutional rights and commitment to statutory enforcement. A typology by Muir (1977) distinguished officers by whether they were comfortable or conflicted about the use of force and whether they had a compassionate or cynical view of the human condition. Chatterton (1983) divided officers between those committed to strict legal and moral standards for arrest and those zealously preoccupied with arrest in disregard of such standards. Brown (1988) developed a four-category typology based on officers' selectivity and aggressiveness in enforcement.

Like the concept of a single police subculture, these personality typologies are also problematic. The classifications were the products of observation rather than analytic procedures such as cluster analysis, and their empirical validity was not subsequently tested (Bailey, 1994; Cochran & Bromley, 2003). Most schemas simply describe officers' preexisting psychological traits, without explaining how these traits may have been shaped by occupational influences. Furthermore, they are overly ridged, failing to account for officers who don't fit neatly into a category or who shift categories (Herbert, 1998).

Some newer studies have addressed these issues. Using statistical methods to develop officer taxonomies, Jermier et al. (1991) found five distinct types of officers: crime-fighting commandoes, crime-fighting street professionals, peace-keeping moral entrepreneurs, ass-covering legalists, and anti-military social workers. Cochran and Bromley's analysis (2003) revealed three law enforcement orientations: subcultural adherents, community-policing practitioners, and "normals" who fit neither category.

These personality typologies better explain the diversity in officer behavior than do the singular prototypes. Occupational traits such as comfort with the use of force and commitment to legality are certainly relevant to arrest-making; "commandos" are undoubtedly more enforcement-oriented than "social workers." But none of the typological schemes recognize predispositions arising *outside* the police identity, or delve into more general characteristics relating to ability and temperament.

What leads one officer to earn extra income through arrest overtime and another to earn that income through moonlighting in a completely unrelated occupation? Why does one officer seek career advancement by amassing an impressive arrest record and another by studying for promotion or attending law school? Answers to such questions involve aspects of the officer's character that go well beyond his or her on-duty personality.

POLICE MOTIVATION

Theories of worker motivation have influenced reform-minded police administrators since the early twentieth century (Fogelson, 1977). Each theoretical trend from scientific management forward has successively made its way into police management texts (e.g., Vollmer, 1936; Smith, 1940; Wilson, 1950; Iannone, 1970; Whisenand, 1981; Leonard & More, 1987; More and Wegener, 1992; Holden, 1994; Roberg and Kuykendall, 1997, Swanson, Territo, & Taylor, 1998; Bennett & Hess, 2007). These theories are arrayed as a progression toward a more humanistic understanding of officers, and a broader appreciation of their environment. Yet, none integrates the influence of private, extra-occupational concerns, despite their tremendous relevance to officer motivation.

Still, many motivational theories discussed in police texts offer insight into self-interested arrest adaptations, even without directly making this connection. For instance, these books present such classic management theorists as Taylor (1916), Fayol (1949), and Weber (1946), who viewed economic incentives as the worker's prime motivator. The classic perspective anticipates the officer who would seek end-of-tour arrests that maximize overtime. Yet if police administration texts mention overtime at all, it is in regard to fiscal management, not officer motivation.

Discussions of police motivation, like overviews of worker motivation generally, have tended to downplay financial motives in their enthusiasm for more "humanistic" outlooks. Most describe the famous Hawthorne experiments that gave rise to the "Human Relations" movement (Roeth-lisberger & Dickson, 1939). These studies were considered the first scientific evidence that workers respond to social incentives, particularly from researchers and coworkers. The Hawthorne employees, organized in teams, controlled production rates through cooperation between more and less skilled workers, and held common agreement to not be a rate-buster, a slacker, or a "squealer." Such peer cooperation has been observed in many police ethnographies, and plays a critical part in how officers coordinate and control arrest-making. Yet police management texts never associate the "universal" attributes of Hawthorne workers and the "subculture" of officers.

From the human relations approach evolved "content" theories of motivation, which related productivity to the fulfillment of human needs. Best known, in both organizational literature and police texts, is Maslow's Hierarchy of Needs (1943). Maslow proposed that individuals, in their many endeavors, must satisfy basic physiological needs, such as sleep, sex, and security, before striving to fulfill higher-order goals such as esteem, personal growth, and self-actualization. His theory would seemingly predict that officers working a double shift, or anticipating a "hot" date, or faced with foreclosure, would make arrest decisions responsive to these "lower" needs. The theory would also predict that officers whose higher needs are more readily satisfied off-duty would avoid arrests in order to spend time on loftier satisfactions. Yet discussions of Maslow in police texts often downplay policing's physical demands, or assume that physiological and security needs are satisfied by a reliable paycheck and pension. The missed meals, lost sleep, and hazardous conditions that officers willingly endure as committed professionals is seldom noted. Such texts rightfully urge supervisors to address officers' higher order needs, but they never acknowledge that officers whose higher-level interests lie outside of work may prefer (and even arrange) a dull, uneventful tour.

Unlike Maslow's model, other content theories presented in police management literature mostly restrict themselves to the occupational environment. For instance, McGregor's Theory X and Theory Y (1960) held that the worker is molded by management assumptions either to become an "X" who resists innovation and challenge, or a "Y" who seeks them out. Policing texts duly recognize that the typical police agency takes a Theory X approach, eliciting minimal, routine work through punitive discipline. The texts fail to consider that this ridged X environment may inspire officers to display Y-style resourcefulness in their patrol behaviors, to accommodate personal goals.

Herzberg's Motivation-Hygiene Theory (Herzberg, 1968) also is specifically aimed at workers. It classifies their concerns as either "hygiene factors" that control worker dissatisfaction, such as salary, job security and working conditions, or "motivators" that provide job satisfaction, such as growth, recognition, and advancement. Though Herzberg's theory is widely cited in organizational and police texts, some have noted its lack of empirical support. For instance, studies have found that a given factor (e.g., working overtime) may satisfy one employee and dissatisfy another, or satisfy and dissatisfy the same employee at different times (Munro, 1974; Wilson, 1989).

Many police management books also discuss Expectancy Theory (Vroom, 1964), which proposes that motivation is the product of the worker's expectation of achieving a given task, the instrumentality (usefulness) of that task in obtaining a reward from management, and the valence, or negative or positive value of each particular outcome. These texts conclude from Expectancy Theory that supervisors should clarify goals and how to achieve them, link the achievement to organizational rewards, and determine which organizational rewards are important to which individuals. Yet police research that applied Expectancy Theory suggests that in practice, officer performance has a very weak link to organizational reward. One study found that over 30 months, as new officers lowered their expectancy that "working especially hard" would lead to organizational rewards, their motivation to work dropped to the level of veteran officers (Van Maanen, 1975). Other research on officers' decisions to arrest drunk drivers found that all organizational rewards for arrest had a negative effect on arrest-making except overtime funding (Mastrofski, Ritti, & Snipes, 1994).

Policing texts eventually progress to Systems Theory (Katz & Kahn, 1966), which advocates openness to the community and responsiveness to external changes. But the implications of an open, adaptive police department are never fully explored. For instance, the increase in police households with single parents or two working parents should lead police agencies to accommodate child-care difficulties of their officers. The competitive job market should spur departments to make police work more attractive—by expanding overtime opportunities, adopting flexible schedules, and revising needlessly aversive procedures. Some departments do indeed offer child-care facilities, flextime, and other family-related accommodations, but the texts fail to link them to Systems Theory.

ARREST DISCRETION

Over a hundred variables have been linked to arrest discretion since its "discovery" by scholars in the 1960s (Smith, 1982; Walker, 1993). The self-interested arrest concerns that are the focus of this study have been missing from that long list. To understand how officers make arrest decisions, we must account for both personal factors and the better-known situational, environmental, and managerial variables.

Writings from the 1960s often viewed police officers as protectors of the socioeconomic status quo, using their discretion to "hold the lid on" societal ills. This sociological perspective of police discretion gained attention through a pioneering field study of criminal justice officials at work began by the American Bar Association in 1956. Among its revelations, wrote research team member Wayne LaFave (1965), is that officers, virtually without legal or administrative restraint, used arrest to address noncriminal problems such as vagrancy, indebtedness, and mental illness. These observations were reinforced by sociologists, particularly conflict theorists who posited that arrests served to impose the social norms of powerful groups upon powerless ones (Turk, 1966; Vold, 1979), and labeling theorists who viewed arrest as part of a ritualized stigmatization that creates a criminal class (Becker, 1963; Lemert, 1967). Ethnographic studies of police lent credence to the view that officers perpetuate the socioeconomic status quo through their discretionary choices (Banton, 1964; Skolnick, 1966; Bittner, 1970; Westley, 1970; Rubinstein, 1973).

This perspective was also supported by quantitative research done in the 1960s and '70s. Studies of arrest decisions established the primacy of legal variables, such as the seriousness of the crime and the willingness of the complainant to prosecute, but they also focused on extralegal factors with sociological implications, such as demeanor, race, class, relationship of suspect and victim, and the type of neighborhood. Many of these variables were integrated by Black (1976) into a theory that the quantity of law (i.e., government control) varies with the level of defiance of social norms. Thus, arrest is most likely for offenses committed against strangers or higher status individuals or in communities lacking informal social control mechanisms.

However, when many of these variables were subsequently reexamined, often using more sophisticated methodologies, the results were far more mixed (Riksheim & Chermak, 1993; Committee to Review Research on Police Policy and Practices, 2004). For instance, the positive relationship between arrest and seriousness of offense has been one of the most consistent findings in the literature (see, e.g., Piliavin and Briar, 1964; Wilson,

1968; Black, 1971, Ericson, 1982; Brooks, 1993). Yet, in some later studies, where seriousness is defined not by the *level* of the charge (e.g., felony versus misdemeanor) but as injuries-versus-no-injuries or weapons-versus-no-weapons, the effects on arrest rates were absent (Berk & Loseke, 1980; Visher, 1983; Smith & Klein, 1984; Worden & Politz, 1984; Bell, 1985; Smith, 1987).

Similarly, most research has found complainant/victim preference for or against arrest to be a significant factor (e.g., Black, 1971; Lundman, Sykes, and Clark, 1978; Berk & Loseke, 1980–1981; Lafree, 1981; Smith, 1984; Worden, 1989; Kerstetter, 1990; Brooks, 1993). However, studies analyzing multiple variables suggest a number of contradictory interactions. For instance, the complainant's preference was more likely to be honored if the offense was minor and if the complainant chose *not* to arrest (Smith & Visher, 1981). Preference had greater effect in lower-status neighborhoods (Smith & Klein, 1984) and homogenous neighborhoods (Smith, Visher, & Davidson, 1984). Female complainants' wishes carried more weight in one study (Visher, 1983) but not another (Smith & Klein, 1984).

The correlation of arrest and citizen demeanor has been another fairly consistent finding. Citizens who were "antagonistic" or "disrespectful" were more likely to be arrested and less likely to be accommodated as complainants than their "civil" or "cooperative" counterparts (see, e.g., Piliavin & Briar, 1964; Petersen, 1972; Sykes, Fox, & Clark, 1976; Lundman, Sykes, & Clark, 1978; Smith & Visher, 1981; Moyer, 1981; Ericson, 1982; Smith & Klein, 1984; Worden & Politz, 1984; Worden, 1989). However, some of these studies have subsequently been challenged for conflating lawful demeanor with conduct that is itself illegal or that occurs subsequent to the moment of arrest (Klinger, 1994; Mastrofski, Worden, & Snipes, 1995).

The effects of many other variables stand unresolved because study results have been contradictory. Race, the focus of much research attention, exemplifies this. Debate surrounding the Black-Reiss data (Black, 1970) focused on whether the higher likelihood of arrests for African-Americans is the result of suspect demeanor or complainant preference, rather than race *per se* (Black & Reiss, 1970; Black, 1971; Lundman, 1974; Lundman, Sykes, & Clark, 1978). Most post-1980 studies, examining a variety of circumstances, concluded that race itself had no effect on police arrest decisions (Berk & Loseke, 1980; Moyer, 1981; Worden & Politz, 1984; Smith & Klein, 1984; Smith, 1984; Smith et al., 1984; Hollinger, 1984; Smith, 1986). Other more recent findings further complicate our understanding, showing, for instance, that whites were more likely to be arrested than blacks if they are physically fighting (Smith, 1986), and that blacks are more likely to be arrested than whites if they are female (Smith & Visher, 1981; Visher, 1983). Also confounding are findings that when the suspect's race is held constant, an arrest is less likely if the *complainant* is black and more likely if white (Lafree, 1981; Smith et al., 1984).

Social class, like race, has a mixed influence. Earlier research found that an arrest was more likely when suspects were lower class (see, e.g., Black and Reiss, 1967; Black, 1971; Reiss, 1971; Friedrich, 1977; Black, 1980), and less likely when complainants were lower class (LaFree, 1981; Smith et al., 1984). Yet a more recent study (Mastrofski et al., 1995) reported that suspect class had no effect.

Studies of suspect age and gender also produced varied results. Juveniles were less likely to be arrested in the 1970s, but were handled more like adults in the "get tough" era of the 1980s, particularly if their offenses were serious (Riksheim & Chermak, 1993; McCord, Wisdom, & Crowell, 2001). Female suspects were sheltered from arrest through the "chivalry" of police officers, according to a number of studies (e.g., Visher, 1983; Mastrofski et al., 1995; Worden, 1995). But again this is too simple; for instance, if the females are juveniles, or defy conventional feminine role expectations, or commit property crimes, they may forfeit this protection (Visher, 1983; Riksheim & Chermak, 1993).

Studies of neighborhood characteristics produced discrepant results as well. Donald Black wrote in *The Behavior of Law* (1976) that poor communities, lacking cohesion and informal social controls, are more subject to the formal controls imposed by police. Yet in subsequent studies, various economic indicators were associated with both higher and lower arrest rates (Liksa & Chamlin, 1984; Smith, 1984; Smith, 1986; Slovak, 1986; Crank, 1990). Community heterogeneity, that is, the level of dissimilarity among residents, had mixed effects (Liksa & Chamlin, 1984; Crank, 1990). The public visibility of police-citizen encounters in a community likewise had varied results (Smith & Visher, 1981; Visher, 1983; Worden & Politz, 1984; Smith, 1987).

Management's level of supervision and policies on arrest can influence arrest behavior. The span of control, that is, the ratio of officers to sergeants, has shown mixed effects on arrest (see, e.g., Slovak, 1986; Crank, 1990), but this indicator offers only a crude approximation of how frequently patrol sergeants are present at potential arrest situations. Reiss (1971) found that close supervision gave officers less of an opportunity to violate department rules, and this presumably would suppress the urge to improperly make or avoid arrests due to personal factors. But patrol work is by nature a "low visibility" activity, that is, it is rarely conducted in the supervisor's immediate presence (Goldstein, 1960; Walker & Katz, 2008).

Management can also increase arrest-making with a determined pro-arrest policy (Sherman, 1990). In a typical "crackdown," orders from the upper echelons are translated almost overnight into street-level arrest quotas. Crackdowns are sometimes short-lived reactions to a particular negative news story, as when, for example, a vicious assault by a stranger on a New York City street prompted a campaign to arrest homeless persons (Bumiller, 1999). At other times, new pro-arrest policies, accompanied by "get-tough" legislative and judicial measures, stem from more fundamental changes in public attitudes. For instance, heightened concern for domestic violence and drunk driving has led many police jurisdictions, including the NYPD, to adopt mandatory arrest procedures (Sherman, 1992; Walker & Katz, 2008).

Perhaps the most unlikely origin for new pro-arrest policies was the *Atlantic Monthly* article, "Broken Windows" (March, 1982), in which James Q. Wilson and George L. Kelling proposed that arrests for "minor" misconduct can dispel the lawless, fearful atmosphere that leads to serious crime. Many departments, including the NYPD, adopted the "Broken Windows" approach (Rosen, 1999; Silverman, 1999). In New York City, the philosophy transmuted into a "Zero Tolerance" policy of escalating low-level arrests, despite flagging statistical justification and community support (Rosen, 1999; Flynn & Rashbaum, 2000).

The managerial approach known as COMPSTAT (short for *Computer Statistics, Comparison Statistics,* or *Computer Comparison Statistics,* depending on the agency) also builds pressure to keep arrests up, and overtime down. Introduced in 1994 to the NYPD and then adopted by other departments, COMPSTAT provides timely data on crime patterns and enforcement activity to middle and top management. The mid-level managers (i.e., heads of precincts and special units) are then expected to monitor emerging problems, devise and implement solutions, and evaluate successes and failures. A key element of this model is the regularly scheduled COMPSTAT meeting. There top police executives examine the statistical data on large-screen projections, and grill middle managers about increased crimes, insufficient arrests, runaway overtime, or other unfavorable trends (Weisburg, Mastrofski, McNally, Greenspan, & Willis, 2003; Committee to Review Research, 2004).

Officers are often aware that the pressure to "produce" is flowing down from these COMPSTAT meetings. One NYPD member reported that his patrol supervisors, and even occasionally his commanding officer, rode in the back seat of patrol cars, directing officers to make arrests.

However, the COMPSTAT *model* is generally not shared with or supported by regular NYPD patrol officers. They are not shown crime data, invited to strategic meetings, or asked for input (Kelling & Sousa, 2001). Department sanctions to meet COMPSTAT objectives do little to motivate them (Eterno, 2003). When crime rates go down, their commanders take the credit while yielding little or none to the rank and file (Eterno & Silverman, 2006). Thus, officers are as likely to resist COMPSTAT goals as to embrace them.

We have seen that in the abundant research on arrest discretion, nearly all the variables examined pertain to the officer's occupational role or work environment. How does this confusing mélange of arrest-related factors inform our study?

First, we observe that many variables are highly reactive; that is, their effects change when other factors are introduced. It would seem unlikely, then, that these well-studied arrest factors would *not* interact with such personal concerns as overtime money, post-work commitments, and arrest processing discomforts.

Second, we should consider that some of the most well-established arrest variables can be manipulated by the officer on a case-by-case basis to further self-interest. The charges against an offender can be trumped up or played down. A complainant's arrest preference can be modified by the officer's biased presentation of the pros and cons of pressing charges. A suspect's demeanor can be altered by the officer's provocative or pacifying comments. Researchers who only consider these familiar variables at the moment of arrest may well be unaware of the officer's prior intervention and motives.

Finally, we should bear in mind that personal incentives may accompany even that most important arrest determinant, the gravity of the crime. True, an officer who arrests a dangerous felon is eager to thwart the criminal and protect the public. But a great collar also brings back-slapping recognition from peers and superiors. It offers a reprieve from the harassment of an overtime-conscious supervisor. And, it provides a strong alibi for broken post-work commitments.

ELEMENTS OF ADAPTIVE ARREST BEHAVIOR

Finally, we come to the components of adaptive arrest behavior directly addressed in this study: overtime, time conflicts, physical and psychological stressors, role conflict, demands on women officers, tour differences, coworker support, arrest-control methods, peer culture and attitudes, and management limitations. A number of studies examine these elements, but few link them to adaptive arrest behavior.

ARREST OVERTIME

In the sparse literature relating personal interests to arrest, overtime money or "collars for dollars," has received the most frequent mention. Van Maanen (1983) reported officers seeking overtime by "engineering" their arrests at end-of-tour and striving for transfer into high-overtime units. Mastrofski et al. (1994), in their study of driving-under-the-influence (DUI) arrests in Pennsylvania, found that a "rate-busting" cadre claimed to enjoy "sticking it" to management with high-arrest overtime costs. The majority of officers in the study criticized the rate-busters as bounty hunters, yet reported that they themselves would increase their DUI arrests if more overtime funding were available. Foley (2000) reported that officers were more likely to lie in stating their grounds for arrest when they needed overtime money.

Only one study was found that empirically correlated arrest with overtime needs. Walsh (1986), comparing officers who made high, medium, low, and no felony arrests in a New York City precinct, found that the high-arrest group is distinguished by a greater dependency on overtime income. Some from this group, which comprised ten percent of all officers but made over half the felony arrests, even characterized themselves as "bounty hunters."

Overtime taken in compensatory time can also be an arrest incentive, particularly if an officer has exhausted his reserve of leave time. Yet in searching the literature on arrest incentives, the only mention of comp time was in a nation-wide survey funded by the National Institute of Justice (Bayley & Worden, 1998). This report discussed comp time in terms of its cost-effectiveness (that is, its loss of man-hours), not its influence on arrest decisions. It also found that many police departments do not even monitor overtime expenses taken in time rather than money.

TIME CONFLICTS

The time burden of arrest processing has been noted by a few authors. Wilson (1968) mentioned extended tours as a possible discouragement to arrest. Forbell (1973) found that officers who faced long commutes make fewer arrests than those who did not, though they were just as active in their other police duties. Vila and Taiji (1999) stated that officers' academic pursuits created a time conflict with arrest processing.

Walsh's study of a New York precinct (1986) found arrest processing length to be a factor in the forty percent of NYPD officers who never processed any felony arrests. This group of officers had the greatest proportion of individuals with off-duty employment and the largest share of wives employed full-time. Walsh reasoned that these officers not only had less need for overtime money but also had greater need to get off work on time, to get to either their second job or their children.

Walsh's study was the only one found that associated arrest avoidance with the common practice of moonlighting. Police officials recognize that while second jobs relieve pressure on their organization to raise salaries, they also sap officers' energy and focus (Krocs, 1985; Violanti & Aron, 1995; Vila & Taiji, 1999). In a poll of police agencies, all reported having written policies on off-duty employment. These include restrictions on the type of work allowed, the maximum moonlighting hours permitted, and the minimum time before and after the police tour that the second job can be scheduled (Sharp, 1999).

The NYPD forbids outside employment that exceeds 20 hours per week or extends within three hours of the officer's start-of-tour, yet it sets no limit on how soon after tour's end the officer may report to a second job. Clearly, even a job beginning three hours after sign-out time would discourage arrest-seeking in the latter half of an officer's tour.

PHYSICAL STRESSORS

The physical difficulties in processing an arrest have received little attention. A study of Canadian officers found that they were deterred from making drunk-driving arrests by the difficulties in controlling intoxicated persons and the distance they had to travel for a breath test (Vingilis, Blefgen, Colbourne, Reynolds, Waslyk, & Solomon, 1986). Similarly, Pennsylvania officers based DUI arrest decisions on such arrest "costs" as effort and unpleasantness (Mastrofski & Ritti, 1992). Conlon's personal account of life as a Housing Police officer described how he would eject but not arrest trespassers who "stank to high heaven" (2004, p. 7).

Yet abundant research, without focusing on arrest, has shown that officers are quite concerned over various physical stressors. These include physical injury, infection, excessive paperwork, and exhaustion (Sykes, Fox, & Clark, 1976; O'Neill & Cushing, 1991; Violanti & Aron, 1995; Barker, 1999; Blumberg, 1997; Vila and Taiji, 1999). Officer fatigue is further exacerbated by outside employment and college attendance (Kroes, 1985; Violanti & Aron, 1995; Vila & Taiji, 1999).

PSYCHOLOGICAL STRESSORS

This same pattern is seen in research on officers' psychological concerns. There is no dearth of research on the sources of mental stress in police work: disciplinary action, civilian complaints, adverse scheduling, strained personal relationships, and possible injury (Kroes, 1985; O'Neill & Cushing, 1991; Violanti & Aron, 1995; Barker, 1999; Bayley & Worden, 1998). Yet only a few studies associate psychological pressures with arrest seeking or avoidance. Mastrofski et al. (1994) found that a significant factor in DUI arrest decisions in Pennsylvania is whether the officer had the training and experience to feel at ease with the work such an arrest entails. Brown (1988) wrote that officers in his California study weighed their fear of making a mistake into their arrest decisions. Hernandez (1981) and Brown (1988) both observed that on slow tours, officers make more proactive arrests for minor offenses to alleviate their boredom or release anger generated in private life.

ROLE CONFLICT

The costs and benefits of arrests are also tied to identities *outside* the police role, such as parent, breadwinner, student, or simply a person of ordinary vulnerabilities. Role conflict between work and non-work identities is well recognized in organizational literature (e.g., Selznick, 1948; Merton, 1957; Kahn, Wolfe, Quinn, & Snoek, 1964; Downs, 1967). But in writings about police, "role conflict" almost always refers to discordant *policing* roles, such as crime fighter, social worker, and peace keeper (e.g., Skolnick, 1966; Wilson, 1968; Brown, 1988; Walker, 1993; Manning, 1997).

Yet the role conflicts between officer and civilian identities may pose the greater threat to the officer's emotional equilibrium. In a study by Kroes, Margolis, and Hurrell (1974), most officers complained that their work interfered with their home life, caused them to lose non-police friends, and made dating difficult to schedule. Maynard and Maynard (1982) and Barker (1999) both reported that over half of married officers in their studies were divorced within their first five years in policing. Territo and Vetter (1981) found that work during evenings, weekends, and holidays resulted in extensive disruption of home life and prohibited the planning of family activities. Clearly, officers hoping to sustain the important personal relationships in their lives would be strongly motivated to exercise "arrest control."

Walsh's study (1986), comparing high- versus low-arrest officers, all male, found a stark difference in their identification with their police and non-police roles. The zero- and low-arrest groups, which comprised 78% of the precinct, were drawn away from their police identities by second jobs and childcare responsibilities left by working wives. Moreover, almost 62% of the zero-arrest officers—the largest category—expressed a desire to retire from the NYPD as soon as they were able, and only 29% expressed a desire to advance within the department. This contrasted with the high-arrest category, which had the highest proportion of married officers but had no wives working full time. Every officer in this group sought career advancement within the department and no one was interested in retirement. Walsh found that all groups but high-arrest reported that they make fewer felony arrests than they could and considered their own preference, not the complainant's, in their arrest decision. This study stands alone in relating family concerns to arrest activity. No research was found that correlated arrest with other outside pursuits such as school or an active social life.

Research on the arrest decision has also neglected the officer's identity as comfort-seeking, pain-avoiding mortal. As shown above, only a handful of studies have actually connected arrest decisions to boredom, or fear of getting hurt or looking foolish. No research was found linking the arrest decision to protracted fatigue or to fear of getting "jammed up" (accused of misconduct) by an arrestee or a supervisor.

SPECIAL DEMANDS ON WOMEN OFFICERS

Despite choosing a "masculine" occupation, female NYPD officers I knew were often as torn between career and family as other working women. The women officers seemed more likely to have sole custody of children, more preoccupied by family matters, more eager to get home on time, more likely to have inside assignments, and more inclined to give away their arrests to coworkers than were their male counterparts. Those female officers who made frequent arrests were rarely primary caretakers of young children.

Women first went on routine patrol in the 1970s, and some studies from that decade indicated that they made fewer arrests than their male counterparts. This disparity may have been caused by their inexperience or disproportionate assignment to inside posts. Later research, which corrected for these factors, found that gender had no effect on arrest behavior (Riksheim & Chermak, 1993; Committee to Review Research, 2004).

Recent studies have also focused on the lack of family-friendly policies in policing. Harrington and Lonsway (2004) wrote that because so many police women are single mothers or are in families with another working parent, child care is often the most critical factor in whether a woman will continue her policing career. It more often is policewomen than policemen who bear the responsibility of nursing a sick family member or simply finding an alternative caretaker at odd hours. Almost no police agencies provide childcare facilities, although such arrangements can work. For example, the Portland, Oregon Police Bureau offers on-site child care at its headquarters and a drop-in child-care facility near the courthouse.

SHIFT DIFFERENCES

The midnight tour has been described as "the Petri dish of police misconduct" (Baker, 2001). In these isolated hours, vice establishments thrive, supervisors are scarce, and officers are conspiratorially close (Lundman, 1980). Over the past three decades, many of the NYPD's most infamous corruption and misconduct scandals have erupted on the midnight shift (Rashbaum, 2008). For the city's officers, arrests on the midnight shift are continuously processed through the day, resulting in maximum overtime. Thus, self-serving arrest-making may be more likely on midnight tours than on other tours.

COWORKER SUPPORT

I initially described how NYPD officers developed arrangements with their coworkers to control arrest-making, albeit with limited success. Officers "learn the job" primarily from colleagues in the field (Rubinstein, 1973; Van Maanen & Manning, 1978), and are taught to value teamwork above individual motivation (Skolnick, 1966; Van Maanen, 1975).

Walsh (1986) found such teamwork in the New York City officers he studied. The no- and low-arrest officers, comprising 78% of the command's patrol strength, were frequently able to give away their arrests to "active" officers—either partners or a "back-up" team. The arrangement kept the squad's arrest average at a satisfactory level and allowed officers to control their occupational environment so as to pursue their personal priorities. Yet because the precinct's felony rate was so high, these accommodations were inadequate. A third of the no-arrest and low-arrest groups (who made fewer than nine arrests per year) admitted to avoiding arrest, and many were thought to have "talked their way out of" them. Active officers complained to their supervisors of colleagues refusing to take their fair share of arrests.

Walsh also found that some officers avoided arrests on holidays. This conforms to my observations that certain events in the calendar inspire such widespread arrest-seeking or avoidance that little cooperation among officers is likely. NYPD arrest statistics do in fact show a marked increase in arrests before Christmas and precipitous decreases on Mother's Day and Super Bowl Sunday—changes that cannot be explained by crime rates alone.

As described earlier, officers seeking arrest may amicably arrange with those avoiding them to be "at the right place, at the right time," should an arrest situation arise. But because those preferring *not* to make an arrest are more plentiful than those who are "looking," an unwanted arrest situation may give rise to protracted arguments as to who should "get stuck."

No study was found that directly examines how the balance of seekers and shirkers affects arrest outcomes. But it would seem that insofar as these groups cannot accommodate one another, officers feel the need to control arrest-making through their patrol tactics.

ARREST-CONTROL TECHNIQUES

In the NYPD, it was apparent that officers adapted their patrol tactics to conform to personal arrest preferences. Other researchers have described similar arrest-control tactics but without necessarily tying the techniques to officer self-interest.

To scrounge up an arrest, officers can focus on vice-prone locales that lend themselves to proactive enforcement (Sherman, 1980; Hernandez, 1981; Brown, 1988). They can postpone informing the dispatcher when their assignment is complete, to make time to pursue a favorite violation (Van Maanen, 1983; Brown, 1988). They can provoke complainants or rile suspects (Walker 1993; Bayley & Garofalo, 1989). To avoid arrest-making, officers can pre-arrange to pass along unavoidable arrests to willing takers (Conlon, 2004). They can drive around with tunnel vision (Brown, 1981), and delay getting to the scene (Walker, 1993; Manning, 1997; Barker, 1999). They can notify the radio dispatcher of their arrival time before or after actual arrival (Manning, 1997), in order to cover a delay or wait for the "catching" sector car. They can spend an inordinate amount of time at service-related assignments (Barker, 1999). In subtle and not-so-subtle ways, they can convince complainants not to press charges (Bayley and Garofalo, 1989; Walker, 1993). They can determine that no crime has occurred and direct complainants to other agencies (Black, 1980; Manning, 1997). They can take a report but never file it or simply not respond to a call (Manning, 1997; Barker, 1999).

PEER ATTITUDES AND CULTURE

The "maxims" quoted in the first chapter suggest that officers rationalize adaptive arrest behavior by both loyalty to outside commitments and disaffection with organizational goals. Many authors have commented on the importance of peer values to police officers (e.g., Wilson, 1968; Van Maanen & Manning, 1978; Lundman, 1979; Bahn, 1984; Dempsey & Forst, 2005). These values are often captured in exchanged "words of wisdom," and serve as the verbal link between ethos and action (Reuss-Ianni, 1983; Kappler et al., 1994).

Admonitions to "Put family first" and to "Make the Job work for you" suggest that the police officer culture endorses withholding some part of one's commitment to "The Job" to affirm one's non-police identity. This tendency of private identities and goals to assert themselves in the workplace has been recognized in organizational writings (e.g., Selznick, 1948; Merton, 1957; Downs, 1967) described previously. Police research, however, mainly explores the opposite vector of influence, that is, how the rigors of the occupation produce a personality and world view that carries over into the private sphere. Officers are described as feeling isolated from larger society and cynical toward police work (Banton, 1964; Skolnick, 1966; Niederhoffer, 1967; Wilson, 1968; Westley, 1970; Van Maanen & Manning, 1978; Burbeck & Furnham, 1985).

As discussed earlier, diversity, steady tours, and other factors have lessened officers' insularity. However, their cynicism still seems to thrive. The often-heard refrain among NYPD officers that "the Job's not on the level" suggests that the officer's turning outward is accompanied by disillusionment. In 1967, officer-turned-scholar Arthur Niederhoffer suggested that police work engenders a cynicism toward both fellow citizens and the agency itself, allowing officers to rationalize illegitimate activities. One common response to this disillusionment is to focus on an activity outside the job (Barker, 1999; Rigoli, Crank, & Rivera, 1990).

Part of the cynicism toward humanity comes with the discovery that arrests can be intrinsically unsatisfying. Complainants may have ulterior motives for pressing charges (Wilson, 1968; Karmen, 2003). Some offenders may not "deserve" arrest because their crimes stem from economic desperation (Conlon, 2004). Repeat arrests of the same individuals may lend an air of absurdity to the whole enterprise (Walker, 1993). Arrests come to be seen not as righteous blows against crime but as just "one of several outcomes" (Manning, 1997).

An added source of disillusionment is the occupational politics that infect the arrest process. Many officers are convinced that connections, not arrests, are the most reliable route to good assignments (Van Maanen, 1975). Officers see that even an exemplary arrest record cannot save a career that high officials one day deem a political liability (Van Maanen, 1975; Wilson, 1989; Guyot, 1991). Officers cynically note how City Hall announces a "crackdown" to counter negative headlines (Wilson, 1989), how police higher-ups manipulate arrest statistics to augment their careers or budgets (Skolnick, 1966; Rubinstein, 1973; Wilson, 1974, 1989; Manning, 1997), how prosecutors plea bargain to assure easy conviction (Arcuri, 1977; Walker, 1993), and how judges hand down lenient sentences to clear court congestion or placate the courtroom "work group" (Arcuri, 1977; Narduli, 1978; Walker, 1993). When officers witness how arrests are subordinated to the self-interest of others, they can easily rationalize manipulating arrests to suit their own priorities.

MANAGEMENT LIMITATIONS TO CONTROLLING ADAPTIVE BEHAVIOR

The arrest motives of NYPD officers can be fairly apparent to precinct insiders. Nevertheless, officers are relatively unconstrained by police management when adapting arrest behavior to personal needs. This is largely due to the awkward realities of first-line supervision, which are documented in business literature (e.g., Kahn et al., 1964) as well as police studies. It is physically impossible for a sergeant to be present at every patrol situation (Banton, 1964; Manning, 1997). Moreover, officers are overtly hostile to being "snoopervised" and second-guessed, which makes sergeants reluctant to respond to too many radio runs (Iannone, 1970; Rubenstein, 1973; Van Maanen, 1983; Brown, 1988; Manning, 1997). Sergeants are psychologically caught between their roles as bureaucrat and colleague and consequently barter favors for work output. These favors include overt assistance to the officers, such as authorizing time off, and more subtle help, such as "not seeing" how certain results are achieved (Van Maanen, 1983; Brown, 1988). The pressure on sergeants to produce "numbers" reinforces this tendency to focus on ends rather than means (Rubinstein, 1973; Van Maanen, 1983). Finally, supervisors need to conserve patrol strength to answer radio assignments. Thus, they may actually discourage officers from making less-serious arrests until nearing the end of tour (Brooks, 1993).

Other problems of control lie with the commanding officer. Police commanders rely on numerical indicators to reveal qualitative information about subordinates (Mastrofski, 1981; Wilson, 1989), even though an unremarkable arrest-making record may merely reflect the balancing out of undesirable arrest-generating and arrest-evading activities. Mastrofski (1981) has suggested that police administrators emphasize statistical records both as a cover for their lack of street-level control of their subordinates and to avoid interference with the officers' actual work in the field, where discretionary latitude is a political and economic necessity. Commanders also respond to the reality that arrest overtime is of concern to their agency only as a budget-buster and not as an arrest incentive. As noted earlier, the 1998 N.I.J. survey of nationwide overtime practices dwelt entirely upon issues of cost-effectiveness (Bayley & Worden, 1998).

WHY ADAPTIVE ARREST BEHAVIOR HAS BEEN OVERLOOKED

Because most research on organizational behavior and motivation is confined to the workplace, it is no surprise that police applications of this research also are restricted to job-related variables. But how is it that studies that directly observe arrest behavior also fail to note the influences of the officer's personal life? Given the volume of such studies, this question must be addressed.

One can look to our larger culture, where the dramatic image of arrest obscures its quotidian realities. This unique authority to use non-negotiable force against fellow citizens is central to our visceral reaction to the officer (Bittner, 1970). Arrests "keep a lid on" society's problems, making the officer a "Rorschach in uniform" for projected grievances (Niederhoffer, 1967; Walker, 1993). Arrests are the "battle statistics" touted by police agencies to rally public support (Smith, 1982; Manning, 1997). Arrests also provide climactic moments in TV and movie entertainment (Kroes, 1985; Holden, 1994). All this takes its toll on objectivity.

In addition, arrest presents tantalizing paradoxes to those of a philosophical bent. It is an unparalleled authority, but it is delegated to modestly educated, entry-level civil servants. It is among democracy's most profound intrusions upon its citizens, yet it is a routine event. It reins in the evildoer but may stigmatize the innocent. It expresses universal morality or indulges private peeves. It furthers justice or perpetuates inequity. Scholars who by nature are drawn to profound issues would have difficulty seeing arrest as determined by a desire to buy a new television or attend a Knicks game.

Perhaps an even stronger factor was the political climate of the 1960s and early '70s, when some of the most influential arrest-related studies were conducted. Many common police practices were declared unconstitutional by the Warren Court. Police abuse of black citizens was officially cited as the spark for race riots in many cities. Radical leaders demonized police and equated the soaring crime rate with political resistance. Officers clashed regularly with student activists, who brazenly broke laws to draw attention to social issues (Walker & Katz, 2007). Academics were in the thick of this ferment—decoding police subculture, advising crime commissions, developing "radical criminology." They were highly unlikely, in these circumstances, to develop a "cop-as-everyman" perspective.

Officers, like their agencies, make little effort to demystify themselves. They resist the deflating truth that they mostly perform service tasks (Reiss, 1971; Brown, 1988; Manning, 1997). According to Skolnick and Woodworth (1967:129), "When a policeman can engage in real police work—act out the symbolic rites of search, chase, and capture—his self image is affirmed and morale enhanced." Goffman (1959) found that most professions highlight their dramatic attributes and conceal activities and motives incompatible with an idealized image. Their "stage" selves present cohesive performances and hide colleagues' errors while their "backstage" selves play out other social realities. Goffman notes that police officers—as well as surgeons, prizefighters, and violinists—have an advantage in displaying their dramatic attributes and concealing what is "out of character," because many of their core work tasks are "wonderfully adapted" to such showmanship.

This self-promotion must be kept in mind when we consider that the many arrest studies originated through systematic social observation (SSO). This method has been criticized for the "reactivity" of officers to the note-taking researchers who walked or rode with them (Committee to Review Research, 2004). Undoubtedly, the observed officers had presented their interpretation of normative police behavior (i.e., "what police are expected to do") and concealed incompatible, extra-occupational concerns. Any discussions of hot dates, dental appointments, and car payments were probably conducted "backstage," that is, out of earshot of the researcher.

Even if some discussion of adaptive arrest behavior were heard, it might not have registered. This is because the major SSO research, such as the President's Crime Commission study (Black & Reiss, 1967), the Police Services Study (Caldwell, 1978), and the Project on Policing Neighborhoods (Mastrofski et al., 1998) used survey instruments that focused on situational, environmental, and organizational variables. The surveys recorded some officer traits such as officer race, education, and experience but left out personal attributes like financial need, family obligations, or personal aversions. And, as these data sets were analyzed and reanalyzed in dozens of subsequent studies, the omissions were replicated.

Thus, a confluence of factors blinded the researcher to the full dimensions of the arrest decision: the culture at large, scholarly attraction to "big" explanations, political climate, officers who only performed "front-stage," and research methods that first omitted personal factors and then fed off the circumscribed data.

CHAPTER THREE

How the Study Was Done

My career-long "field study" of New York City police officers persuaded me that arrest decisions are heavily influenced by personal needs—needs that originate *outside* the police identity. Yet, no previous research had ever described this phenomenon, or quantified its elements. Obtaining such personal information would require anonymously questioning the officers themselves.

The survey developed for this study (Appendix B) has 84 items, some of which presented a series of related questions. These delved into the officers' family structure, work situation, financial needs, time constraints, perceptions of arrest processing, attitudes toward arrest-making, and the importance of personal concerns relative to other arrest-making factors. Most of the items offer scalar selections—either integers from zero to ten, percentages at 10% increments, or ordinal selections such as "Never" through "Always." Other items provide categorical choices or solicit word or numerical fill-ins. Many sections offer the officers space for comment.

OBTAINING THE SAMPLE AND SUBGROUPS

Securing the Police Department's permission to conduct the survey required no fewer than eight endorsements "through channels," from commanding officer up to police commissioner. The endorsements reveal how the components of a single vast agency can have divergent goals: The Deputy Commissioner of Legal Matters warns that the study "must not conflict with [Lt. Linn's] duty to report misconduct" revealed by any "identified UMOS," and questions whether the survey is worth the cost in "paid police hours" (Linn, 2004, p. 232). In contrast, the Deputy Commissioner of Policy and Planning, who heads the NYPD's "think tank," requires proof of approval from the "University's Human Subjects Committee" (which obliges me to protect subjects from adverse outcomes), and asks to be fully apprised of the study's results (Linn, 2004, p. 233).

The survey was administered during In-Service Tactical (IN-TAC) Training, a mandatory two-day course that every service member in the rank of police officer and detective attends once a year. Most of the IN-TAC attendees are the regular "street cops" assigned to the Patrol Bureau, while a few participants patrol public housing projects as part of the much smaller Housing Bureau. (Transit Bureau officers, who patrol subway and bus lines, train separately and did not participate in the survey.)

Time for the survey was set aside on the second IN-TAC day, when the training schedule was lighter. (In fact, some instructors expressed appreciation that the survey helped the day pass more quickly.) Each patrol command was proportionally allotted a set number of IN-TAC seats to fill each weekday and selected from among officers scheduled to work until everyone has attended.

Of some concern are officers who miss IN-TAC training because they are on sick leave, or who avoid a schedule change to day tour because it conflicts with personal time commitments. Also absent from the sample might be those who have new arrests or court appearances. Thus, the least active and most active officers might be undercounted. Still, each command makes an effort to catch up with these officers, yielding a fairly representative sample.

All seven of the IN-TAC sites designated for Patrol and Housing Patrol Bureau training were included in the study. These sites served the eight NYPD Patrol Boroughs as shown in Table 3-1.

Table 3 -1. *Survey Sites*	
Location	*Patrol Borough Served*
New York State Armory, 2366 5th Ave	Manhattan North
Police Academy, 235 E. 20th St.	Manhattan South
PSA #3, Flushing & Central Ave.	Brooklyn North
69th Pct., 9720 Foster Ave.	Brooklyn South
D.O.T. Bldg., 92-33 168th St.	Queens North & Queens South
49th Pct., 2121 Eastchester Rd.	Bronx
Petrides School, 715 Ocean Terrace	Staten Island

The surveys were administered on twenty-seven dates between April 12, 2002 and June 21, 2002, usually at two sites per day. The class sizes ranged from six to thirty-four officers. Visiting dates for the sites were selected so as to maintain proportions of participants from each Patrol Borough similar to those found in the Department as a whole. The schedule was then adjusted on the day before an intended visit, because personnel shortages at officers' commands sometimes forced IN-TAC instructors to cancel the session due to low attendance, or to hold class with as few as five officers. Very small classes were avoided when possible, as they were inefficient and diminished the participants' sense of anonymity. As Table 3-2 shows, geographic representation ultimately came within three percentage points of each borough's combined Patrol Bureau and Housing Bureau figures (NYPD, 2003, March 3).

Table 3-2. *Borough Distribution of Officers: Full Sample vs. NYPD Patrol and Housing Bureaus*

Borough	Sample N	Sample %	NYPD N	NYPD %
Manhattan	205	31.3%	4,586	28.2%
Brooklyn	196	29.9%	4,926	30.3%
Queens	123	18.8%	3,067	18.8%
Bronx	110	16.8%	3,031	18.6%
Staten Island	21	3.2%	666	4.1%
TOTAL	655	100%	16,276	100%

It could be ascertained from the Sign-in Logs maintained at each IN-TAC site that 42 of the 716 officers who attended were from non-patrol units such as Organized Crime, the Police Academy, the Court Section, and Support Services. Though some of these 42 chose to complete questionnaires, none were included in the study. This left 674 attendees eligible to participate in the survey. Of these, 655 officers, or 97.2%, filled out questionnaires. This sample represents about 4% of the approximately 16,000 officers assigned to the Patrol and Housing Patrol Bureaus (NYPD, April 11, 2003). These 655 survey-takers are referred to as the *Full Sample.*

Among the 655 in this Full Sample were two overlapping groups of officers who were outside the central focus of this study. First, there were the "House Mice," those officers assigned to non-patrol positions such as community affairs, crime analysis, captain's clerical, and other administrative posts. These 95 officers were separated based on Questionnaire Item 5, wherein they reported going on patrol twice a week or less. The second group eliminated comprised officers who were not in a position to make autonomous arrest decisions because they worked as part of a team, accompanied by a sergeant. These 74 "Team Players" were separated if they reported in Questionnaire Item 6 that in a typical week they were assigned at least once to Anti-Crime, Street Narcotics Enforcement, Field Training, or other team arrangement. Thirty officers fell into both the House Mice and Team Player groups, so that a total of 139 officers were removed.

What remained was a *Core Sample* of 506 participants: officers who performed regular uniformed patrol, alone or with a partner, with relative autonomy, at least three out of five days a week. They are the focus of most of the analyses in this study, as they make the vast majority of arrest decisions. From the Core Sample, several subgroups were also identified by arrest rate, gender, and borough. Table 3-3 summarizes the selection criteria for the groups analyzed in this study.

Table 3-3. *Derivation of Full Sample, Core Sample, and Subgroups*

Group	N	Selection Criteria	Item #
Full Sample	655	IN TAC attendees from patrol commands who prepared surveys	5, 6
Core Sample	506	FS officers who patrol alone or with partner, 3 or more times/wk.	5, 6
No-Arrest	151	CS officers who made no arrests in the previous month	10
High-Arrest	95	CS officers who made 3 or more arrests in the previous month	
Males	379	CS officers who are male	74
Females	68	CS officers who are female	
Midnights	88	CS officers from CS working 1st Platoon, 11:05 pm–7:40 am.	4
Days	173	CS officers working 2nd Platoon, 7:05 am–3:40 pm.	
Evenings	171	CS officers working 3rd Platoon, 3:05 pm–11:40 am .	
Bronx	79	CS officers from slowest-processing major borough, the Bronx.	top[a]
Queens	103	CS officers from quickest-processing major borough, Queens.	

[a] Borough of assignment was written in after questionnaires were collected.

Table 3-4. *Personal and Family Characteristics of the Core Sample* (N=506)			
Age	Range	Mean	SD
	21–55	31.9	5.6
		N	Valid %
Gender	Males	379	84.8%
	Females	68	15.2%
Race/ Ethnicity	White	247	63.0%
	Black	39	9.9%
	Hispanic	94	24.0%
	Asian/Indian	8	2.0%
	Other	4	1.0%
Education	HS Diploma	48	10.7%
	Some college, no degree	158	35.1%
	Associate Degree	102	22.7%
	B.A./B.S.	127	28.2%
	Some grad school, no degree	10	2.2%
	M.A./M.S.	5	1.1%
	J.D./PhD.	1	0.2%
Living with Parents	Yes	91	20.0%
	No	363	80.0%
Living with Spouse/ Partner	Yes	252	56.0%
	No	363	44.0%
Living with Special-Needs Adult	Yes	13	3.1%
	No	401	96.9%
Living with another Adult Caregiver	Yes	28	6.8%
	No	381	93.2%

PERSONAL CHARACTERISTICS AND FAMILY LIFE

To understand how private motives affect arrest behavior, we need more personal information than the usual demographic data on age, sex, and race. Table 3-4 summarizes such characteristics, as reported in Survey Items 74–83.

Several personal and family characteristics have ramifications for arrest behavior. For example, 45.8% of Core participants do not have the 64 college credits that would be required for promotion to sergeant. In order to rise in rank, these officers would need to attend college, and would have to control their work schedule to accommodate their classes.

About 43% of participants' households include children and/or dependent adults. Their needs may well conflict with the post-tour demands of police work, particularly among the 10.5% of such households where there is no spouse or live-in partner.

Less than 7% of those with children at home say they live with another adult caregiver, such as a home attendant, nanny, or other relative. Asked to elaborate, 14 of 16 respondents describe childcare arrangements that involve extended family. It may be that modest salaries or difficult hours limit the professional childcare options available to most officers.

Household composition differs by gender, as shown in Table 3-5. Female officers are considerably *less* likely to have a spouse or partner and *more* likely to have children at home. Moreover, only about two-thirds of the female households with children also have a spouse or partner, while nearly all of the male households with children also have a spouse or partner. It might be expected, then, that the childcare concerns would weigh more heavily on the minds of Core Group women than men.

Table 3-5. *Household Composition of Male and Female Officers in Core Sample*							
"Yes" Responses	Total	Males	Females	Df	X^2	V	P
Living with Spouse/ Partner	248 (56.4%)	218 (58.3%)	30 (45.5%)	1	3.76	.092	.053
Living with Children	178 (40.2%)	147 (39.0%)	31 (47.0%)	1	1.49	.058	.223
Living with Spouse/Partner & Children	160 (90.4%)	139 (95.2%)	21 (67.7%)	1	22.21	.354	<.001

This demographic portrait suggests several sources of conflict between officers' arrest-making and the demands of their personal lives. These demands are examined more directly in the other survey items.

ADMINISTRATION OF THE SURVEY

Because officers traditionally greet inquiries about their methods with a "blue wall of silence" (Westley, 1970; Geller, 1997; Walker & Katz, 2008), special efforts were made to secure participants' cooperation. First, the IN-TAC instructor at each site introduced me in his or her own words, always mentioning my rank (I was dressed in civilian clothes). I then personally distributed the surveys and read aloud the written introduction, "Information for Participants in this Study" (Appendix B).

The introduction provided a consistent presentation that served several functions. It assured participants that the questionnaire, while appearing long, required only about thirty-five minutes to complete. It tied the survey to the widely studied subject of police discretion, implying that such research is common and not a threat to participants. It gave advance notice that the officers would be asked personal information. It pointed out several safeguards to their anonymity, including the absence of specific identifiers among the survey items and the procedure to return competed surveys in sealed envelopes and in random order. The introduction emphasized that the study is not sponsored by the Police Department but rather is affiliated with John Jay College of Criminal Justice, a well-known local institution. Finally, it offered several ways for officers to directly contact me.

The participants were also told to help themselves at any time to refreshments (coffee, juice, bagels with cream cheese, fruit, cookies, and donuts) set up on a table in the classroom. These items were jokingly referred to as "the bribe," and they indeed seemed to buy the officers' good will.

Participants were allowed up to one hour to complete the survey. They reached the end of their 16-page questionnaire at a rate of better than 90%, despite being asked over 250 items of personal information. For most survey items, there were fewer responses than the totals shown in Table 3-3. In presenting findings, the upper-case N denotes the number of participants in the Full Sample or Core Sample who provided answers to the item(s) under discussion. The lower-case n refers to the number of subgroup participants (drawn from the Full or Core Samples) who answered the item(s).

WERE THE RESPONSES VALID?

Before administering the survey at IN-TAC, it was vetted by the City University of New York's Institutional Review Board and by four members of CUNY's Criminal Justice doctoral faculty. The instrument was also reviewed by the National Science Foundation, which awarded funding (Grant #0136630/01).

In addition, several officers who expressed interest in the study had previewed the survey and given their reactions. While recognizing that these officers may be atypical, I was encouraged by their positive reactions. They reported that they understood all the questions, and did not find the survey to be overly long. Asked if they found any portion to be offensive, they said that to the contrary, they were pleased to be asked about the frustrations of arrest processing and hoped the Department would pay attention to their responses. No officer objected to my seeing the completed survey, though told that it need not be returned.

Still, it is inevitable to wonder whether the participants would respond honestly. The questions touch upon many sensitive issues: To what extent are arrest decisions made before an incident even occurs? What personal concerns give rise to a need for overtime money, schedule control, or evasion of arrest-processing burdens? By what means, and how often, are arrests actively sought or avoided? How is self-interested arrest behavior privately rationalized? How important are personal concerns compared to other arrest factors? How effective is management in controlling adaptive arrest behavior?

As the individual who administered every survey, I believe I was able to assure participants that their identities would remain secret and that the research was intended not to disparage officers but to address their grievances. However, even when a questionnaire is anonymous and completed in good faith, participants are tempted to give socially desirable responses (Babbie, 2007). In this study, the officers may well have distorted some answers to appear a bit more conscientious and unbiased, and a bit less swayed by personal interests, than they actually were. Even so, the information they reveal is sometimes unflattering, and hardly conforms to our ideals of just, professional arrest-making. It should be taken seriously by anyone interested in the welfare of officers, the cost-effectiveness of police work, or the fairness of arrest decisions.

CHAPTER FOUR

Patrolling and Arresting

(Survey Items 1–20)

For a majority of police officers on patrol there is always someone "looking" when the second half of the tour starts… Many guys have families and depend on this arrest overtime.

Participant 268

Officers must arrest serious offenders and meet expectations for "arrest productivity," yet still maintain enough control of arrest-making to accommodate personal needs. Several factors enhance officers' ability to manage their arrests. They must have the patrol experience to know how to find an arrest and how to avoid one. They need cooperative coworkers, in particular their patrol partners. They must have a good sense of timing in order to anticipate illegal conduct and maximize arrest overtime.

As is typical of patrol officers, most of the Core Sample are at the front end of their twenty-year police career, with a mean of 6.1 years on the job ($SD = 4.97$, $N = 500$). The newest officer has ten months with the Department, and the most senior has close to 21 years. The mean time that participants are at their present commands is 4.9 years ($SD = 4.11$, $N = 497$). Forty-eight officers, or 9.7%, have been at their present commands for their entire career. Participants generally view their command's crime level as being moderately high, rating them on a zero-to-ten scale at 6.2 ($SD = 2.17$, $N = 503$).

Most officers are assigned to one of the three basic platoons (sometimes referred to as midnights, days, and evenings) as indicated in Table 4-1.

Table 4-1. *Usual Tours of Core Sample* (N = 506)			
Tour	*Hours*	*N*	*Valid %*
1ˢᵗ Platoon (midnights)	11:05 p.m. to 7:40 a.m.	88	17.6%
2ⁿᵈ Platoon (days)	3:05 p.m. to 11:40 p.m.	173	34.7%
3ʳᵈ Platoon (evenings)	11:05 p.m. to 7:40 a.m.	171	34.3%
Community Policing/Other	Various	67	13.4%
Total		499	100%

All 506 participants, in qualifying for the Core group, report three or more patrol assignments per week; 423, or 83.6%, reported going on patrol every day.

By examining how frequently the participants go on patrol, we can see that women officers patrol less frequently than men. The non-Core group of 149 officers, who mostly patrol less than three times per week, is 39.2% female; the Core Sample is 15.2% female. Table 4-2 compares the assignments of 655 male and female officers in the Full Sample.

Table 4-2. *Gender and Frequency of Assignment to Patrol for Full Sample* *(N = 655)*							
Frequency and Valid Percent within Gender							
	Rarely/ Never	1x/ mo-/ 1x-wk	2x / Week	3x / Week	4x / Week	≥5x / Week	Total[a]
Male	12 (2.6%)	20 (4.3%)	16 (3.5%)	28 (6.0%)	37 (8.0%)	350 (75.6%)	463 (100%)
Female	7 (6.5%)	15 (14.0%)	9 (8.4%)	10 (9.3%)	7 (6.5%)	59 (55.1%)	107 (100%)
Total	19 (3.3%)	35 (61%)	25 (4.4%)	38 (6.7%)	44 (7.7%)	409 (71.8%)	570 (100%)

Note X^2 (5) = 28.973, V = .225, $p < .001$.
[a] Includes full sample of 655 officers, comprising Core & Non-Core Groups. Percentages may not equal total due to rounding.

There are clearly different rates of assignment to patrol for male and female officers, with the disparities most pronounced at the extremes. For instance, 6.9% of males versus 20.5% of females report that they go on patrol once a week or less, while 75.6% of males and 55.1% of females report patrolling five times per week or more. Cumulatively, only 71.1% percent of female officers from the Full Sample meet the Core Sample criterion of three or more patrol days per week as compared to 89.6% of men.

The lower proportion of women on patrol has several possible causes. It may be due in part to supervisors' belief that females are less suited to the physical demands of patrol—a belief reported in a number of studies. However, the NYPD does have strong anti-discrimination procedures that could be invoked (or merely threatened) if the disparity in assignment is pronounced. The disproportion may also reflect supervisors' assumption that females possess superior office skills (although the women surveyed did not have more education than the males). A disproportionate female preference for the predictability of non-patrol assignments may well be another factor, given that 32% of women officers are single custodial parents, as compared to 5% of the men.

Core participants are also asked to list their assignments in a typical five-day week. Table 4-3 first presents the Core Sample's seven most commonly named assignments, which accounted for 87.6% of responses. Included in "Other Posts" are over 40 additional positions, each under 2% of the total.

All seven posts of the most common posts entailed patrol. The mobile, two-officer Sector Car, comprising two-thirds of assignments, may be the most "arrest-prone" unit because it is usually the first to be assigned to crimes in progress and is ultimately responsible for taking any unavoidable, unwanted arrest in its geographic sector. Other named assignments offer varying odds for arrest making. The solo Foot Posts rarely are first on the scene, but they are sometimes assigned to take low-level arrests in order to keep the Sector Cars rolling. The Conditions Auto, like the Sector Car, responds to 911 calls but does not have primary responsibility in any particular sector. The SP 10 Car officers respond mostly to past or non-emergency incidents and thus encounter fewer potential arrest situations. The Sergeant's or Lieutenant's Operator is expected to drive the supervisor for the entire tour and seldom makes arrests.

Table 4-3. *Core Sample Assignments Over 5-Day Period* (N = 506)		
Assignment	*Times assigned over 5-Day Period*	*% of all Responses*
Sector Car	1683	66.5%
Foot/Summons	204	8.1%
Patrol	74	2.9%
Conditions Auto	66	2.6%
Sgt./Lt. Operator	58	2.3%
SP 10 Car	55	2.2%
Car/RMP	52	2.1%
Other Posts	313	12.4%
Total	2530[a]	100%[b]

[a] All 506 participants reported 5 days of assignments; 506 x 5 = 2530.
[b] Sum of individual assignment percentages may not equal percentage total due to rounding.

Arrest-making is easier for officers to control when they have a steady partner with compatible arrest-making inclinations. Of Core participants, 73.2% report working with a regular partner at least three times a week, 62.2% has the same partner at least four times a week, and 52.8% has the same partner for five days a week ($N = 500$).

Officers may have two approaches to "partnering up." They might choose coworkers who are like themselves in arrest-making style. By doing so, laid-back partners would guarantee each other an uneventful tour, while aggressive partners would take turns "collaring up" and reaping the overtime. This type of pairing would conform to my informal observation that patrol partners have generally similar approaches and attitudes toward police work. The second possibility would be for officers to choose their opposites, so that when an arrest is made, it would be handled by the partner hungry for overtime and not by the partner eager to leave work on time or avoid the processing ordeal. To determine which approach is more common, participants are asked how many arrests in the previous month were made by partners.

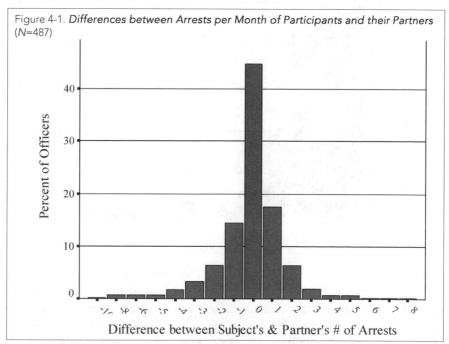

Figure 4-1. *Differences between Arrests per Month of Participants and their Partners* (*N*=487)

Percent of Officers

Difference between Subject's & Partner's # of Arrests

Figure 4-1 shows the distribution of differences when partners' arrests are subtracted from participant's arrests. Most often the pairs match each other in number of arrests. Only 10.5% of officers report an arrest-making disparity greater than two. This suggests that officers choose partners with similar inclinations to make or avoid arrests, rather than those with opposite but complementary arrest-making goals.

Though the vast majority of daily assignments offered arrest opportunities, Core participants report a mean of only 1.6 arrests in their last full month worked (SD = 1.9). The distribution is quite skewed, as depicted in Figure 4-2. Specifically, 30.2%, or 151 officers (the No-Arrest group) report zero arrests, and another 29.8%, or 149 officers, report one arrest. Only 94 officers, or 18.8%, make three or more arrests (the High-Arrest group), but they are responsible for about 54% of all arrests.

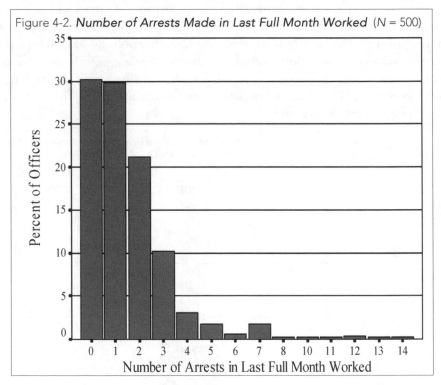

Figure 4-2. *Number of Arrests Made in Last Full Month Worked* (N = 500)

Male and female Core participants who patrol regularly report statistically equal arrest rates. Interestingly, had this same comparison been made for the Full Sample, policewomen would average significantly fewer than the men—1.2 arrests (SD = 1.2) as opposed to the male average of 1.6 (SD = 1.9: t (233.17) = 2.938, p = .004.) This is apparently because the Full Sample includes those who patrol under three times per week, a group that is disproportionately female. Thus, the disparity in arrest rates between females and males among officers in general appear to be the result of different rates of assignment to patrol, not different patrol behaviors.

Among the 86.6% of the Core group who worked the midnight, day, and evening tours, there are no significant differences in arrest rates. However, among the different boroughs of the city (Table 4-4), arrest rates vary significantly; $F(4, 495) = 2.914$, $MSe = 3.488$, $p = .021$. The highest arrests per month, 2.1, are in the Bronx, the borough most associated with high crime and poverty. The lowest arrest rate, 1.1, is in Staten Island, the borough with half the Bronx's crime rate and the feel of suburbia. There are significant differences between arrest rates in Manhattan and Queens, the Bronx and Brooklyn, and the Bronx and Queens. Staten Island showed no statistical difference from the other boroughs, probably due to its small number of survey participants.

Table 4-4. *Arrests per Officer in Last Full Month Worked in the Five New York City Boroughs* (N = 506)

Borough	N	Mean	SD
Bronx	79	2.1	2.0
Manhattan	154	1.7	2.3
Brooklyn	152	1.5	1.7
Queens	103	1.2	1.2
Staten Island	12	1.1	1.1
Total	500	1.6	1.9

The low rate of arrest does not appear to be related to a lack of arrest opportunities. Asked to rate the difficulty of finding an arrest, from 0 (*usually very easy*) to 10 (*usually very hard*), respondents produce a mean rating of 4.1 ($SD = 2.4$), suggesting that they find it somewhat easy. Figure 4-3 presents the distribution of scores, indicating that 48.1% of the officers give "easy" ratings of 4 or lower, while only 25.3% give "difficult" ratings of 6 or higher. Not even the No-Arrest group reports arrest-finding to be hard, rating the mean difficulty level at 4.9 ($SD = 2.6$, $n = 147$). However, the High-Arrest group rated arrest-finding almost two points easier, at 3.1 ($SD = 2.3$, $n = 95$). This difference is significant; $t(240) = 5.389$, $p < .001$.

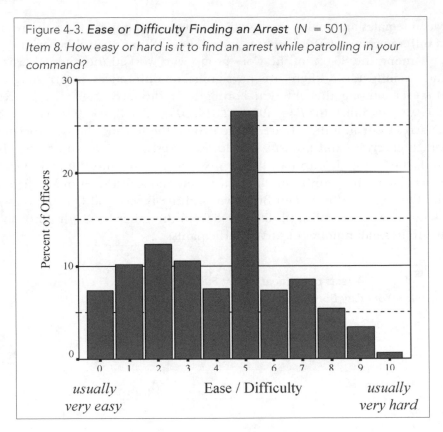

Figure 4-3. *Ease or Difficulty Finding an Arrest* (N = 501)
Item 8. How easy or hard is it to find an arrest while patrolling in your command?

A need for overtime money would logically be an incentive for patrol officers to make arrests. Yet at the time of the survey officers had considerable overtime opportunities from other sources, such as the special enforcement initiative CONDOR (Citywide Organized Narcotics Drug Operational Response) and the many post-9/11 security details. Table 4-5 compares these various overtime sources, indicating that routine arrest-making is an inferior source of overtime in terms of both the percentage of officers involved and their average monthly earnings.

The Core Sample shows a strong inclination to take their time-and-a-half overtime in money rather than time. Asked to select to the nearest 10% the *time* portion of their overtime, participants average 18.9% of overtime in time instead of cash (*SD* = 25.6, *N* = 503). This preference may reflect not only a need for cash but the abundance of vacation time (at least twenty-five days per year) afforded to NYPD officers.

Table 4-5. *Sources of Overtime*

Source	N respond-ing	N getting OT from source	% getting OT from source	Mean OT hrs/month for those getting OT from source	SD
Routine Arrest Making	497	264	53.1%	10.9 hrs.	11.1
Other Sources (a & b):	484	321	66.6%	22.5 hrs.	25.5
a) Special Enforcement	491	159	31.8%	15.9 hrs.	11.5
b) Security / Special Events	489	275	56.0%	18.8 hrs.	24.7

Note. Participants may report more than one overtime source.

One obvious way to increase overtime is to make arrests for less-serious offenses as close as possible to the end of the tour. If officers ignore this reality, they would make arrests at a fairly even pace throughout their workday. As Table 4-6 indicates, within the second half of their workday, participants make about half their arrests, as would be expected. But in the last hour, they make 25.1% of their arrests, more than double the 12.5% that would be anticipated in one out of eight hours of patrol.

Table 4-6. *Percent of Arrests Made in 2nd Half and Final Hour of Tour*

			2nd Half			
Item 18. About what proportion of your arrests are made in the **second half** of your tour?						
N	Mean % in 2nd Half	Expected Mean %	SD	T	Df	Sig.(2-tailed)
495	50.8%	50%	25.6	.66	494	>.05
			Last Hour			
Item 19. About what proportion of your arrests are made in the **last hour** of your tour?						
N	Mean % in 2nd Half	Expected Mean %	SD	T	Df	Sig.(2-tailed)
499	25.1%	12.5	25.3	11.15	498	<.001

The arrest-making is even more accelerated among the High-Arrest group, which makes 27.5% of arrests in the final hour ($n = 92$, $SD = 26.3$). The No-Arrest group also prefers final-hour arrests, but to a significantly lesser degree, making 20.4% of their arrests at that time ($n = 150$, $SD = 23.5$); t (176.58) = -2.11, $p = .036$. This suggests that the desire for overtime influences last-hour arrest-making, particularly among those who make a lot of arrests.

What then do we learn about adaptive arrest behavior from these responses? First, officers overall choose to make relatively few arrests, though they find it fairly easy to find someone breaking the law. Second, routine arrests provide only half as much overtime as other sources. Third, officers usually work with steady partners who have a similar arrest-making approach, and this facilitates arrest control. Fourth, overtime may be an incentive to postpone arrest making until the end of tour.

The high-arrest officers find it easier to catch lawbreakers. Perhaps because they have honed this skill, they are better at timing their arrests at the very last hour than the average Core group officer.

Women hold a higher proportion of arrest-proof inside assignments. The reasons for this are not clear, but one indirect factor may be the greater demands on them as (often single) parents. When female officers go on patrol as often as males, as part of the Core Sample, they make the same number of arrests.

CHAPTER FIVE

Pre-Incident Proclivity

(Survey Items 41–55)

When my babysitter can spend the night I will try to collar, if not then I try to avoid arrests.

Participant 218

Having confirmed one observation—that officers postpone arrest-making until the end of their tours—we now examine what takes place at the beginning of their shift. This is when officers discuss their arrest-making intentions. The next section of the survey seeks to measure the extent to which arrest outcomes correspond to the officers' pre-arrest plans and patrol behaviors. It has two parts, the first focusing on the participants' most recent arrest and the second focusing on their most recent rejection of an arrest opportunity. Each part first presents questions to assure that the arrest outcomes to be examined are recent and freely chosen. It then examines the officers' pre-incident intent, using two criteria: whether they began their tour with a desire to make an arrest and whether they are in "looking" (arrest-seeking) mode while on patrol.

MOST RECENT ELECTIVE ARREST

Only arrests made within 90 days of completing the survey are examined, so that officers' memories will be reasonably accurate. The arrests to be considered also have to be freely decided rather than forced on the officer by a supervisor, a mandatory arrest policy, or some other inescapable circumstance. Thus, of the 424 arrests made within the time frame, only 264 (62.3%) have no supervisor at the scene from the outset. Of these, only 89 arrests (33.7%) are *not* procedurally mandated or otherwise unavoidable. This final sample of 89 *elective arrests* therefore represents 21.0% of arrests made in the previous 90 days. An elective arrest in this context is one in which the officer has a *de facto* choice.

The 89 arrests were made, on average, 24.3 days earlier ($SD = 18.2$). The offenses involved, as written out by the participants, appear in Table 5-1. Fifteen of the arrests are for felonies, 49 are for misdemeanors or violations, and 25 could be either for misdemeanors or felonies.

Participants are asked to rate their pre-tour arrest intentions, from 0 (*strongly didn't want an arrest*) to 10 (*strongly wanted an arrest*). The distribution of pre-tour preference scores is illustrated in Figure 5-1. It shows that at the beginning of their arrest-making tour, 14 officers (15.7%) did not want an arrest, 48 (53.9%) had no preference, and 27 (30.3%) wanted an arrest. It also reveals a ten-officer group (11.2%) who had the most extreme desire to make an arrest. The mean pre-tour arrest preference score is 5.6 (SD = 2.3), a small but significant elevation over the mean of 5 that would be expected if the officers had no pre-tour preference; t (88) = 2.517, p = .014. In other words, when officers make elective arrests, they tend to start their workday in favor of that decision.

Table 5-1. *Offenses Reported in Elective Arrests* (n = 89)			
Assault	13	Attempted Kidnapping	1
Driving without License	12	Public Lewdness	1
Petty Larceny	7	Crim. Possess. of Forged Instrument	1
Trespass/Criminal Trespass	7	Unlicensed Vendor	1
Assault 2nd Degree	4	Trademark Counterfeiting	1
Crim. Possess. of Controlled Substance	4	Window-Washing	1
Burglary	4	Outstanding Warrant	1
Disorderly Conduct	4	Misdemeanor	1
Robbery	3	Criminal Contempt	1
Menacing	3	Auto Theft	1
Driving While Intoxicated	3	Unauthorized Use of Vehicle	1
Criminal. Mischief	3	Harassment	1
Assault 3rd Degree	3	Assault-Family Offense	1
Rape	2	Larceny —Family Offense	1
Criminal Possession of Weapon	2	Unspecified	1
Note. If participant reported more than one offense, the first one listed is shown.			

This is supported by a comparison with the pre-tour preference scores of the 329 officers who made arrests with the supervisor present or under procedurally mandated or otherwise unavoidable circumstances. This "non-elective" group averaged a significantly lower arrest preference of 4.6 (*SD* = 2.6); *t* (416) = 3.49, *p* = .001. Thus, unlike the elective-arrest officers, the non-elective officers start their tours with a desire to *avoid* arrest.

To determine if those who make elective arrests consciously patrol in an arrest-seeking mode, participants are asked to describe their pre-arrest patrol activities, from 0 (*trying hard to avoid an arrest*) to 10 (*trying hard to make an arrest*). Figure 5-2 shows that before the incident, seven officers (7.9%) were trying to avoid an arrest, while 20 (22.4%) are trying to make one.

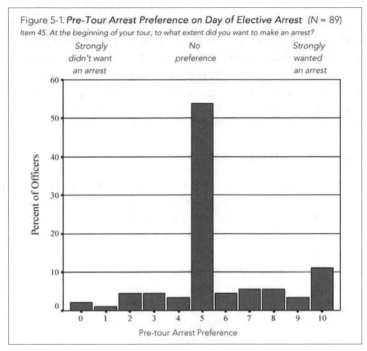

Figure 5-1. *Pre-Tour Arrest Preference on Day of Elective Arrest* (N = 89)

Item 45. At the beginning of your tour, to what extent did you want to make an arrest?

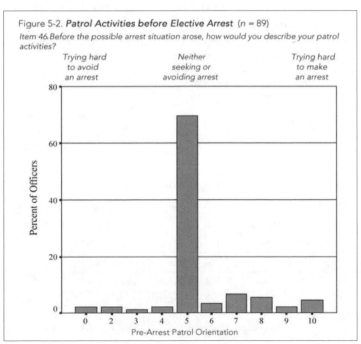

Figure 5-2. *Patrol Activities before Elective Arrest* (n = 89)

Item 46. Before the possible arrest situation arose, how would you describe your patrol activities?

A large majority of 62 officers (69.7%), are neutral in their patrol orientation. The mean score is 5.4 (*SD* = 1.7), again, a slight but significant increase over the expected mean of 5, were officers *not* trying to engineer a specific patrol outcome; *t* (88) = 2.34, *p* = .022. Thus, the elective arresters are actively looking for an arrest. However, they are looking only slightly harder than the non-elective officers, whose mean patrol-seeking orientation is 0.2 points lower at 5.2 (SD = 1.6)—an insignificant difference: *t* (414) = -1.02, *p* = .308.

MOST RECENT DECLINED ARREST

The survey next queried officers about their most recent arrest opportunity that was "shitcanned," that is, disposed of. Of 205 possible arrest incidents ending *without* arrest in the previous 90 days, 140, or 68.3%, had no supervisor at the scene. For this final sample, the arrests were declined, on average, 15.0 days earlier (*SD* = 17.6).

Shown in Table 5-2 are the offenses involved in the 140 declined arrests as described by the officers. Three of the incidents (burglary, auto theft, and possession of a forged instrument) are felonies, 75 concern misdemeanors or violations, 49 can be either felonies or misdemeanors, and 13 are not described. As one would expect, there is a far smaller proportion of felonies in this list than in the list of arrest-bound incidents (Table 5-1). On the other hand, many of the same misdemeanors and violations appear in both tables; that is, the same minor offenses sometimes lead to arrest but more often do not.

Table 5-2. *Offenses Reported in Declined Arrests* (*n*=140)			
Assault	33	Minor Violation	2
Driving without License	17	Security Holding	2
Trespass/Criminal Trespass	9	Criminal Possession of Controlled Substance	1
Larceny	8	Burglary	1
Criminal. Mischief	7	Disorderly Conduct	1
Domestic (unspecified)	7	Public Lewdness	1
Harassment/Agg. Harassment	6	Criminal Possession of Forged Instrument	1
Criminal Possession of Marijuana	4	Unlicensed Vendor	1
Driving While Intoxicated	4	Counterfeit CDs	1
Drinking in Public/Open Container	4	Criminal Contempt	1
Menacing	3	Auto Theft	1
Public Urination	3	Unnamed/Missing	13
Warrant	3		
Note. If participant reported more than one offense, the first one listed is shown.			

Participants are asked to recall their pre-tour arrest intentions on the most recent day they declined an arrest. The distribution of pre-tour preference scores, in Figure 5-3, shows that at the start of their tour, 67 officers (47.9%) did not want an arrest while 12 (8.6%) wanted one. Thirty-two officers (22.9%) select the extreme avoidance score of 0 and with the 61 "no preference" officers (43.6%) create a bimodal distribution. The mean pre-tour arrest preference score is 3.4 (SD = 2.6), a marked decrease from the mean of 5 that would be expected if the officers have no prior inclination; t (139) = -7.43, p = .001. Thus, when officers decline an arrest opportunity, they tend to begin their workday already disinclined to arrest.

Officers are then asked to rate their pre-declination patrol activities, to determine if they are consciously trying to evade arrest. Figure 5-4 indicates that 47 officers (33.8%) are patrolling in "avoidance mode" to some degree, while 10 (7.2%) are "looking," that is, trying to make an arrest. The largest group of 82 officers (59.0%) is patrolling with no particular orientation. The mean rating is 4.1 (SD = 2.06), which, if compared to the

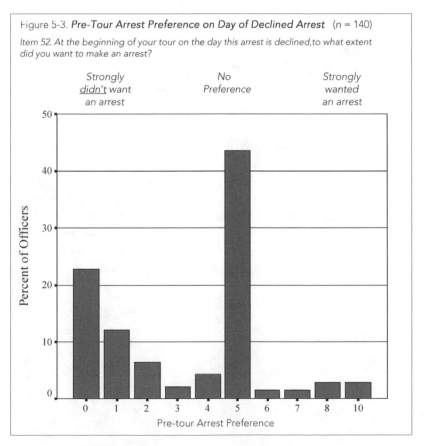

Figure 5-3. *Pre-Tour Arrest Preference on Day of Declined Arrest* (n = 140)

Item 52. At the beginning of your tour on the day this arrest is declined, to what extent did you want to make an arrest?

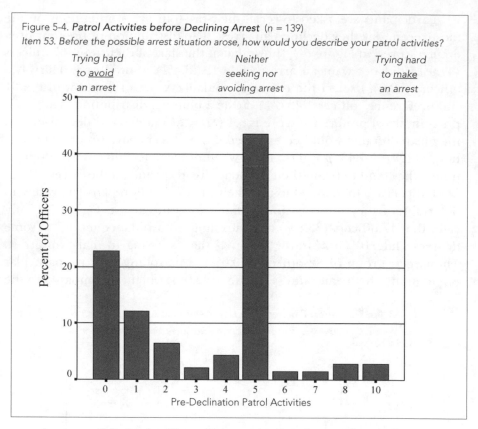

Figure 5-4. *Patrol Activities before Declining Arrest* (n = 139)

Item 53. Before the possible arrest situation arose, how would you describe your patrol activities?

neutral score of 5, is significantly more inclined toward avoiding arrest: t (138) = -5.18, $p < .001$

One concern when asking busy officers to recall events up to three months prior is that they may telescope the time frame or not remember accurately. With that caveat, the responses suggest that when officers freely choose to make or decline arrests, their decisions are not merely influenced by on-the-scene variables. They tend to favor the eventual arrest outcome from the very start of their tour and to patrol in a manner likely to bring about that outcome.

CHAPTER SIX

Officers' Money

(Survey Items 20–23)

This department gives us a "cap" on the overtime but allows you to do more overtime for arrest. If an officer is hurting for money and must make an arrest to make money, the department is encouraging violations of people's civil rights. We should be allowed to make unlimited hours of overtime if we are not going to get a decent wage.

Participant 27

Officers who frequently bring in arrests are kidded by their peers and scrutinized by their superiors for making "collars for dollars." What *is* the role of money in arrest decisions? Do high-arrest officers find it harder than others to make ends meet on their basic salary? Do they have less income from alternative sources, such as a working spouse (as Walsh found in his study)? Do they seek arrests because they have fewer opportunities for *non*-arrest overtime? And do officers on the whole seek more arrest overtime when they have greater expenses, less outside income, and fewer overtime alternatives?

MONEY ISSUES IN CONTEXT

Officers' views on their income must be understood in the context of New York's recent history. At the time of the survey (April through June, 2002), the NYPD was in the midst of long and bitter salary negotiations. The City's flush economy had just taken a dive. The aggressive department initiative, CONDOR, compelled thousands of officers to make arrests on overtime tours. Then on September 11, 2001, the World Trade Center was attacked.

By the spring of 2002, officers had been working without a contract for almost two years. In the past decade, their work had helped bring about an unparalleled 27% drop in crime in New York (Walker & Katz, 2008). Tourists flocked to the city, and its economy flourished (Greenhouse, 2000, July 29). Yet under the last five-year contract, which had expired in July 2000, Mayor Rudolf Giuliani had deferred pay raises for two years. As Patrolmen's Benevolent Association President Patrick Lynch would repeatedly declaim, "We brought crime down double digits and how are we paid? With double zeros!" (Cardwell, 2001).

The NYPD's starting base pay was $31,305 (plus about $4000 in overtime and night differential), and reached $55,268 in base salary after 20 years (Greenhouse, 2000). In comparison, officers in neighboring Newark, New Jersey earned about 39% more (Weiss, 2001). Nassau County, just east of New York City, started officers at $5000 below the NYPD, but paid up to $100,000 annually after five years. And in Suffolk County, east of Nassau, new officers received about $45,000 and reached an average of over $80,000 annually (De la Cruz, 2000). Many New York City officers lived in Nassau and Suffolk, and were galled to see their suburban counterparts making a lot more money for a lot less work.

Moreover, it was substantially more expensive to live in or around New York than in most areas of the country. For instance, in the first quarter of 2002, Manhattan's cost of living was 119% higher than the national average, Queens was 33.4% higher, and adjoining Nassau County was 37.9% higher (Council for Community & Economic Research, 2002).

The PBA began negotiating a new contract in the summer of 2000 with a media blitz aimed at garnering public support. Television and subways ads, some deemed too graphic to run, featured images of a police officer lying bleeding next to his patrol car (Rashbaum, 2000). A series of full-page ads in metropolitan newspapers urged people to *not* join the Department:

> In your first year as a New York City police officer, you will risk your life every day... reduce crime to its lowest level in decades... be among the lowest paid law enforcement professionals in the country (De la Cruz, 2000).

The Giuliani administration responded with a proposal that the city's 27,000 police officers *give up* two weeks' pay over the first year of any new contract, to be recouped upon retirement. Union leaders condemned the plan, saying it would amount to an effective four percent cut in pay. The city then suggested that it was willing to increase pay by 2.5 percent annually or more if the union made concessions on so-called productivity issues. The PBA held to its demand for a 39 percent raise over two years, to bring salaries in line with those in Newark (Greenhouse, 2000, July 29).

By year's end, negotiations were at a stalemate, with each side accusing the other of using feints and public relations ploys to avoid serious negotiations. The PBA filed a notice of impasse, in which it sought the appointment of a mediator to enter the talks. But the two sides could not even agree on whether mediation agencies for the city or the state would intervene (Flynn, 2000, December 19). The PBA continued to press its case at a boisterous rally near City Hall in January 2001. Thousands of angry officers filled four city blocks, waving signs such as "No increase in pay, no reason to stay," and "To make ends meet, I mow a Nassau cop's lawn" (Cardwell, 2001).

But by the spring of 2001, the nation's economic downturn reached New York City. Revenues from businesses declined steeply. The vast pension fund, much of it invested in the once-booming stock market, rapidly shrank. New cost-of-living adjustments raised payouts to the city's retirees (Cooper & Lipton, 2002). Operation CONDOR (Citywide Organized Narcotics Drug Operational Response) had cost the city an extra $100 million in police overtime in the past year (Flynn, 2000).

Then, on September 11, 2001, the attack on the World Trade Center drove the city into a deeper recession than the nation. The New York Stock Exchange was closed for four days. Plane flights were suspended and then avoided, hurting the airline industry, local businesses connected to it, and tourism. As large downtown businesses remained closed or relocated, the small businesses that served them were painfully affected. The city lost 94,700 jobs in October and November alone (Cooper & Lipton, 2002).

Twenty-three NYPD members lost their lives when the Twin Towers collapsed. Thousands more started working twelve-hour tours for as many as seven days a week. Some officers continued to work overtime details at Ground Zero, bridges and tunnels, city landmarks, and other sensitive locations, through the time of the survey. As New Yorkers gradually regained some sense of normalcy, they openly expressed gratitude toward the police in the media, at public events, and in their everyday contacts with officers. The union saw an opportunity to finally persuade the city to atone for past stinginess. "Zeros for Heroes" became the new slogan. Yet when Mayor Michael Bloomberg took office in January, 2002, facing a $4.76 billion budget deficit, he promptly announced that the City's latest pay offer of a ten percent increase over the next two years was all the city could afford (Baker, 2002).

Though CONDOR and the World Trade Center attack depleted the city's budget, both tended to reduce officers' desire for routine arrest overtime. Officers who made CONDOR arrests felt less administrative pressure and economic need to arrest on an ordinary workday, and after repeated compulsory tours, they urgently wanted to end their regular shifts on time. Similarly, the World Trade Center attack offered enormous amounts of overtime to officers, but drained them emotionally and physically. The desire for routine arrest overtime was replaced by the desire to simply go home, shower, and sleep. Moreover, the post-9/11 weeks were marked by lower crime rates, as even habitual offenders seemed subdued by the tragedy.

As the two sides finally began legally binding arbitration hearings before a state panel in March 2002, the NYPD made plans to cut overtime by two-thirds in the coming fiscal year (Flynn, 2002). Thus, when officers took the survey, they were facing fiscal pressure to reduce their demands, a recent surfeit of overtime, and tight scrutiny of their overtime earning.*

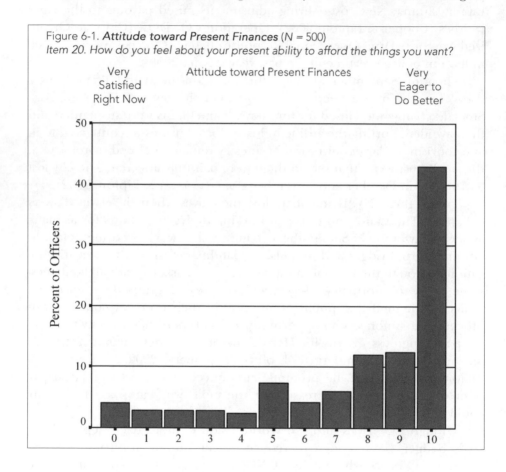

Figure 6-1. *Attitude toward Present Finances* (*N* = 500)
Item 20. How do you feel about your present ability to afford the things you want?

*The new contract was finally settled in September 2002. Officers were awarded an 11.7 percent raise over 24 months, with no "givebacks" in leave time (Greenhouse, 2002). But the new NYPD recruits would finance the deal, receiving a starting salary of only $25,100 per annum—promptly leading the Department and PBA to accuse each other of "eating their young."

FINANCIAL NEED

When the officers are asked to rate their ability to afford the things they want (Figure 6-1), from 0 (*very able right now*) to 10 (*very eager to do better*), the respondents' mean rating is 7.7 (*SD* = 3.0), with 43.0% choosing the extreme score of 10. No-Arrest and High-Arrest officers expressed no significant difference along this scale.

Another element of officers' financial situation is the extent to which they have other sources of household income, such as a second job, spouse's salary, military service, rental income, parental assistance, and so forth. The Core Sample's mean for such outside sources is 29.4% of total income (*SD* = 28.1). No-Arrest and High-Arrest officers displayed no statistical differences in mean percentage of outside income. And, as Figure 6-2 shows, for 34.4% of households the police salary is the *sole* source of income. Thus, for the typical officer, the police paycheck appears to be a critical determinant of financial well-being.

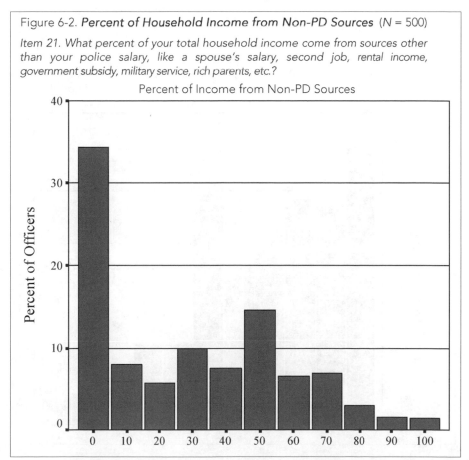

Figure 6-2. **Percent of Household Income from Non-PD Sources** (N = 500)

Item 21. What percent of your total household income come from sources other than your police salary, like a spouse's salary, second job, rental income, government subsidy, military service, rich parents, etc.?

Percent of Income from Non-PD Sources

Officers' perceived need for arrest overtime may also be related to the adequacy of non-arrest overtime. As was shown in Table 4-5, about two-thirds of officers earn overtime from sources outside routine arrest-making, averaging about 23 overtime hours per month, as compared to only about half that number of officers earning routine arrest overtime and averaging just 16 hours per month. Yet when asked to rate the sufficiency of these alternative overtime opportunities, from 0 (*Never Enough*) to 10 (*Always Enough*), participants express their discontent with a mean score of 3.2 (*SD* = 2.6). Figure 6-3 shows that the most frequent response, from 17.8% of respondents, is 0, or "Never Enough." Statistically similar scores are reported by No-Arrest and High-Arrest groups.

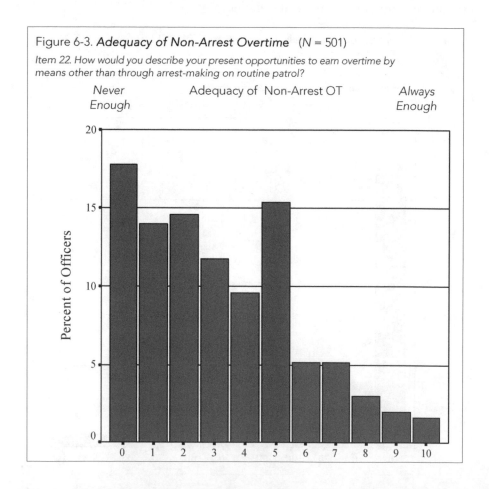

Figure 6-3. *Adequacy of Non-Arrest Overtime* (*N* = 501)

Item 22. How would you describe your present opportunities to earn overtime by means other than through arrest-making on routine patrol?

Having reported overall dissatisfaction with their police income, critical dependence on that income, and inadequacy of overtime sources outside routine arrest, officers are asked a final financial question, about their need for overtime money from arrests made on routine patrol. In a range from 0 (*Never any real need*) to 10 (*Always a great need*), the mean response

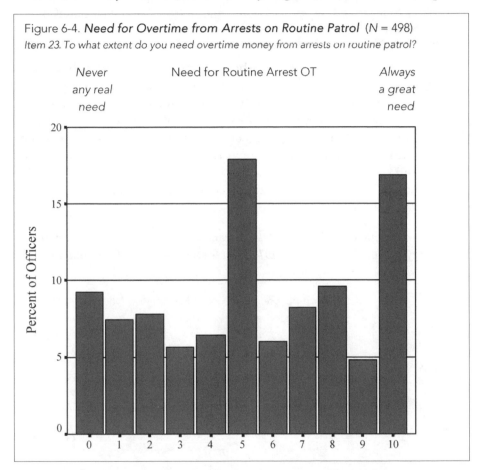

Figure 6-4. **Need for Overtime from Arrests on Routine Patrol** (N = 498)
Item 23. To what extent do you need overtime money from arrests on routine patrol?

is a slightly needy 5.4 (*SD* = 3.3). Figure 6-4 shows a bimodal pattern of answers, with 17.9% of officers selecting a noncommittal midpoint of 5 and 16.9% selecting the extreme score of 10.

The No-Arrest officers congregate on the low-need side of the scale, with a mean score of 4.5 (*n* = 148, *SD* = 3.3), while the High-Arrest officers are a full two points higher, at 6.5. (*n* = 93, *SD* = 2.8) This disparity is significant; *t* (220.642) = -5.02, *p* <.001. Thus, we see that No- and High-Arrest officers differ in their perceived need for routine arrest overtime even though they are alike in financial satisfaction, outside income, and opportunities for non-arrest overtime. One possible explanation is that officers who make arrests on a regular basis quickly develop a dependency on their overtime-enhanced paychecks. Participant 117 expressed this view:

> Twenty percent of the cops in every command make all the collars. I bet if you look at their personal lives, they are the ones living beyond their means. If processing and court were streamlined, you'd see the "do nothings" come to life and the so-called "good cops" go dead.

For the Core participants as a whole, those who are more dissatisfied with their present finances (i.e., more *eager to do better*) experience a greater need for arrest overtime. Officers who feel their non-arrest overtime sources are less adequate also express a greater need for overtime through routine arrest-making. Officers' outside income, however, is not related to arrest overtime need in any predictable way. Perhaps this is because outside income, as from a second job or a working spouse, can both signify financial need and alleviate it. A correlation matrix (Table 6-1) displays these relationships:

Table 6-1. *Correlation of Financial Dissatisfaction, Non-PD Sources of Income, Adequacy of Non-Routine-Arrest OT, and Need for Arrest OT on Routine Patrol* (N = 506)

		Non-PD Sources of Income	Non-Routine-Arrest OT	Need for Arrest OT on Routine Patrol
Dissatisfaction with Present Finances	r	-.09*	-.18**	.26**
	n	494	497	494
Non-PD Sources of Income	r		.01	.07
	n		497	494
Non-Routine-Arrest OT	r			-.29**
	n			497

* $p \leq .05$.   ** $p \leq .01$.

Table 6-1 also indicates small but significant negative relationships between financial dissatisfaction and outside income and between financial dissatisfaction and adequacy of overtime from non-arrest overtime sources. In other words, officers who feel more strapped financially are slightly more likely to have secondary income and to be wanting more non-arrest overtime.

What then, can we say about officer finances as an arrest incentive? First, officers feel a large gap between what they want and what they can afford. Second, because 70% of their families' income comes from their police paychecks, those paychecks are critical. Third, while officers get the greater part of their overtime from sources other than routine arrests, they still consider these sources to be insufficient. Fourth, though most officers have a moderate need for routine arrest overtime, a distinct segment of participants rates their need for arrest overtime at the maximum level.

Officers' need for overtime from routine arrests is significantly correlated with financial dissatisfaction and the adequacy of other overtime sources. However, arrest overtime need shows no relationship to outside income.

No-Arrest and High-Arrest officers are statistically alike in their desire to better themselves financially, in the proportion of their household income coming from non-policing sources, and in the insufficiency of alternative overtime opportunities: These economic circumstances thus appear unrelated to arrest *rates*.

However, the need for overtime from routine arrests is significantly greater for the High-Arrest officer. Because the High-Arrest group seemed to have economic circumstances similar to the No-Arrest group, the High-Arresters' perceived need for arrest overtime may stem from a dependency on their overtime-enhanced paychecks that develops when they begin making arrests on a regular basis.

Officers clearly would like to make more money, but given their low overall arrest rates, they seem more inclined to respond to arrest's major *disincentives*: time constraints and aversive processing. These are examined next.

CHAPTER SEVEN

The Pull of Personal Life

(Survey Items 24–31)

If I had to travel anywhere on my RDOs, plans of that nature would greatly affect my arrest-making decisions.

Participant 271

My wife has to work to help out and I struggle with childcare and my children's school work. Therefore I sometimes have to decline or avoid arrests so I can take care of my other responsibilities.

Participant 470

Making no arrests because of a second job or school is not completely recognized by the department because they don't understand that you have a life outside this job.

Participant 448

How can we measure the impact of officers' private lives on their arrest decisions? Personal commitments, such as to family, school, a second job, social events, and other appointments, may have the *general* effect of requiring the officer's time whenever that time can be spared, thus broadly discouraging any extension of the workday with an arrest. These same commitments, along with commuting difficulties, may also have the *specific* effect of demanding the officer's time right after a given tour, so as to directly induce the officer to avoid a delayed sign-out. In the survey, officers are asked how often these various personal concerns created a general and a specific time constraint. They are then asked how frequently these concerns, taken together, make them feel obligated to end their tour on time.

Table 7-1, concerning general time constraints, and Table 7-2, concerning specific time constraints, compare the Core Sample's monthly or weekly frequency of each concern. In the last column is a *Time Constraint Index* for the specific activity, derived by first assigning a point value to each frequency level (*Rarely/Never* = 0, *1-4x/month* = .5, *1x/week* = 1, *2x/week* = 2, etc.). That point value is then multiplied by the percentage of officers engaged in the activity at the respective frequency level, and the products are added across the row. Thus, the maximum possible Index score for each activity, if 100% of officers selected the *5x/week* category, would be 500. Activities are listed in the table from highest to lowest Index scores.

Table 7-1 suggests that care of children and family makes the greatest general demand on officers' time. Fully one-quarter of officers are caregivers for five or more days per week. Dates or social engagements and other appointments are closely rated in second and third place. Much lower scores are given to the general time constraints of a second job and school.

Table 7-1. **Personal Commitments and Need to Leave Work in General** (N = 506)
Items 24–30. About how often do you [attend to your commitment] in general?
A. Rarely/Never; B. 1-4 days /month; C. 1 day /week; D 2 days /week; E. 3 days /week;
F. 4 days /week; G. 5 or more days/week

| Commitment | N | Number and Percent of Officers Engaged in Activity in General | | | | | | | General Time Constraint Index [a] |
		Rarely/ Never	1–4x / Month	1x/Week	2x/Week	3x/Week	4x/Week	5x/Week	
Care for Children/Family Members	504	214 (42.5%)	58 (11.5)	14 (2.8)	33 (6.5%)	47 (9.3%)	11 (2.2%)	127 (25.2%)	184
Dates/Social Engagements	504	53 (10.5%)	168 (33.3%)	66 (13.0)	97 (19.2%)	75 (14.9%)	27 (5.4%)	18 (3.6 %)	152
Other Appointments	502	57 (11.4%)	195 (38.8%)	71 (14.1%)	87 (17.3%)	49 (9.8%)	15 (3.0%)	28 (5.6 %)	138
Second Job	499	332 (66.5%)	55 (11.0)	16 (3.2%)	36 (7.2%)	29 (5.8%)	10 (2.0%)	21 (4.2%)	70
School/School Assignments	501	428 (85.4%)	13 (2.6%)	14 (2.8%)	18 (3.6%)	14 (2.8%)	5 (1.0%)	9 (1.8%)	33

[a] Row sum of (Percent of Officers Engaged in Activity) x (Times per Week). Rarely/Never scored as 0, 1x/wk scored as 1, 2x/wk scored as 2, etc. Maximum possible. General Time Constraint Index score is 500.

The low impact of second jobs and school was surprising. It is possible that the recent abundance of overtime stemming from CONDOR and 9/11 may have discouraged officers from engaging in both outside employment and school. It also may be that, of the 35% of participants with some college credits but not enough for promotion, many postpone a return to school until they learn that they passed the sergeant's exam. Often promotions are delayed by law suits and appeals over specific test questions, so that at least a year goes by before even the exam's top scorers get their sergeant's stripes. Thus there is enough time for those lower on the promotional list to earn a few more credits.

Table 7-2 compares those activities most likely to take place *within three hours after the end of tour* and to thereby create a "must leave" mindset. Here, the Post-Tour Time Constraint Index reveals that concerns over commuting home far outweigh all others. Caring for children or dependent family members follows as an important post-tour time constraint, while appointments, social engagements, second jobs, and school are substantially less important.

Table 7-2. *Personal Commitments and Need to Leave Work within Three Hours after Tour* (N=506)

Items 24–30. About how often do you [attend to your commitment] within 3 hours after your tour? A. Rarely/Never; B. 1- 4 days /month; C. 1 day /week; D 2 days /week; E 3 days /week; F. 4 days /week; G. 5 or more days/week

Commitment	N	Number & Percent of Officers Engaged in Activity 3 Hours Post-Tour							General Time Constraint Index[a]
		Rarely/Never	1–4x /Mo	1x/Wk.	2x/Wk.	3x/Wk.	4x/Wk.	5x/Wk.	
Commuting Concerns	504	208 (41.3%)	38 (7.5%)	18 (3.6 %)	27 (5.4 %)	37 (7.3%)	25 (5.0%)	151 (30.0%)	210
Care for Children/ Family Members	494	268 (54.3%)	43 (8.7%)	18 (3.6 %)	17 (3.4 %)	34 (6.9%)	9 (1.8%)	105 (21.3%)	149
Other Appts.	487	167 (34.3%)	138 (28.3%)	65 (13.3%)	53 (10.9%)	41 (8.4%)	7 (1.4%)	16 (3.3%)	97
Dates/Social Engagements	489	180 (36.8%)	130 (26.6%)	62 (12.7%)	56 (11.5%)	40 (8.2%)	10 (2.0%)	11 (2.2%)	93
Second Job	479	389 (81.2%)	20 (4.2%)	10 (2.1%)	21 (4.4%)	21 (4.4%)	7 (1.5%)	11 (2.3%)	44
School / School Assignments	484	431 (89.0%)	13 (2.7%)	8 (1.7 %)	12 (2.5%	8 (1.7%)	5 (1.0%)	7 (1.4%)	24

[a] Row sum of (Percent of Officers Engaged in Activity) x (Times per Week). *Rarely/Never* scored as 0, *1x /wk* scored as 1, *2x /wk* scored as 2, etc Maximum possible Post-Tour Time Constraint Index score is 500.

The widespread concern over commuting home from work is probed in a separate question, summarized in Table 7-3. There we see that 314 participants report time-related commuting concerns, of which the vast majority is car-related.

Table 7-3. *Commuting Concerns of Core Sample* (*N* = 506)
Item 29. Do you have any of the following commuting concerns when leaving work?
A. a car pool; B. beating rush hour; C. catching train/bus/ferry; D. other (describe)

Responses	# of POs	%
Time-Related Concerns:	314	62%
Car Pool	24	5%
Beating Rush Hour	217	43%
Catching Train / Bus / Ferry	49	10%
Other Time-Related Concerns (e.g.,):	48	9%

- Choosing the right route due to construction
- Driving too far because I cannot afford to live closer
- Falling asleep at the wheel
- Finding street parking after midnight
- If I work OT after 4x12, I have to take the subway at 2 or 3 am. It's horrible, and there's a good chance of running into a perp that I arrested.
- Getting to babysitter's house in time to pick up children
- Only 1.5 hours to get to second job
- Just wanting to go home

Non–Time-Related Concerns	17	3%
No Commuting Concerns Indicated	173	34%

Note. Participants could indicate any number of Time-Related and Non–Time-Related Concerns or not indicate any concern

The final survey item about time constraints asked officers how often *overall* they feel they must end their tour on time (and, implicitly, must avoid an arrest) because of *any* of the listed commitments or concerns. Table 7-4 indicates that almost two-thirds of all participants feel they cannot extend their tour on one or more days per week. Over one-fourth of officers feel that they can *never* extend their tour.

Table 7-4. *Overall Need to End Tour on Time*
Item 31. Overall, how often do you feel you must end your tour on time because of any of the above commitments or concerns?

Never/ Rarely	1–4x/ Month	1x/ Week	2x/ Week	3x/ Week	4x/ Week	5x/ Week	Total
109 (21.6%)	79 (15.7%)	21 (4.2%)	46 (9.1%)	70 (13.9%)	46 (9.1%)	133 (26.4%)	504 (100%)

Officers in the No-Arrest group feel the need to leave work on time significantly more often than officers in the High-Arrest group, as shown in Table 7-5.

Table 7-5. *Overall Need to End Tour on Time for No-Arrest and High-Arrest Officers*

Item 31. Overall, how often do you feel you must end your tour on time because of any of the above commitments or concerns?

Group	Never/ Rarely	1–4x/ Month	1x/ Week	2x/ Week	3x/ Week	4x/ Week	5x/ Week	Total
No-Arrest	34 (22.5%	19 (12.6%)	7 (4.6%)	8 (5.3%)	22 (14.6%)	16 (10.6%)	45 (29.8%)	151 (100%)
High-Arrest	22 (23.4%)	22 (23.4%)	5 (5.3%)	11 (11.7%)	13 (13.8%)	7 (7.4%)	14 (14.9%)	94 (100%)

X^2 (6) = 13.174, V = .232, p = .040

Table 7-6. *Correlation between Officer Commitments and Need for Timely End of Tour*

Commitment		Need for Timely EOT	
		r_s	N
Commuting Concerns	within 3 hours of end of tour	.44***	502
Care for Children / Family Members	generally	.30**	503
	within 3 hours of end of tour	.35***	493
Other Appointments	generally	.25***	501
	within 3 hours of end of tour	.30***	486
Dates/Social Engagements	generally	.18***	503
	within 3 hours of end of tour	.23***	488
Second Job	generally	.12**	498
	within 3 hours of end of tour	.21***	478
School / School Assignments	generally	.078	500
	within 3 hours of end of tour	.09*	483

* Correlation is significant to .05 level (2-tailed).
** Correlation is significant to .01 level (2-tailed).
*** Correlation is significant to .001 level (2-tailed).

Table 7-6 shows significant positive correlations between Core officers' personal commitments and their perceived need to end their tour without delay. Not surprisingly, activities scheduled for within three hours after tour are always more closely associated with the desire to leave work than the same activities engaged in generally.

Commuting, the most common of the post-work time concerns (see Table 7-2), is also the issue most highly correlated with the need for a timely end of tour. Commuting problems thus may have a chronic suppressing effect on non-critical arrests, given the facts that dense traffic and road construction are endemic to New York City and that officers are allowed by long-standing NYPD policy to reside in remote counties.

The correlation between care of dependent family members and sign-out need is second-highest, both in general and within three hours of the end of tour. This too has broad implications for arrest-making, given the extent of childcare obligations (see Tables 3-4 & 3-5). The next highest correlation, both generally and three hours post-tour, is between other appointments and sign-out need. These non-social appointments, such as going to the dentist, may have less of an impact on arrest making, because they are relatively infrequent (Tables 7-1 & 7-2). Slightly lower still are the correlations of post-tour dates or social events and post-tour second jobs with sign-out need. Here too, their low general and post-work frequencies (Tables 7–1 & 7-2) may help explain their decreased correlation with sign-out need. Involvement in college bears the smallest relationship to sign-out need and is significant only when within three hours post-tour. To summarize, all personal commitments except the general time constraints of school are linked to officers' professed need to sign out on time.

Table 3-5 indicated that proportionally more female officers than male officers lived with children, and that these females living with children are far less likely to have a spouse or partner at home than are the males living with children. This supports a prediction that female officers will more frequently need to take care of children or dependent family members, both in general and within three hours post-tour.

Table 7-7 bears this out. The cross-tabulations show, for instance, that generally, 20.1% of male officers versus 47.1% of female officers provide five-day-a-week care for family members. Within three hours post-tour, 16.3% of men as opposed to 45.5% of women provide this daily care. Values for Chi-square and Cramer's V demonstrate significant gender differences in family-related commitments, particularly post-tour.

Table 7-7. *Gender and Family Commitments*

Item 24. How often do you have to take care of children or dependent family members…(a)…in general; (b)…within 3 hours after your tour

In-General Number and Valid Percent within Gender (N=447)

	Rarely/ Never	1x–4x/ Month	1x/ Week	2x / Week	3x / Week	4x / Week	≥5x / Week	Total
Male	171 (45.1%)	45 (11.9%)	12 (3.2%)	26 (6.9%)	40 (10.6%)	9 (2.4%)	76 (20.1%)	379 (100%)
Female	21 (30.9%)	7 (10.3%)	1 (1.5%)	4 (5.9%)	2 (2.9%)	1 (1.5%)	32 (47.1%)	68 (100%)

Post-Tour Number and Percent within Gender (N=440)

	Rarely/ Never	1x–4x/ Month	1x/ Week	2x / Week	3x / Week	4x / Week	≥5x / Week	Total
Male	211 (56.4%)	36 (9.6%)	15 (4.0%)	11 (2.9%)	33 (8.8%)	7 (1.9%)	61 (16.3%)	374 (100%)
Female	28 (42.2%)	4 (6.1%)	0 (0%)	2 (.3%)	1 (1.5%)	1 (1.5%)	30 (45.5%)	66 (100%)

Note. For General Commitments, X^2 (6) = 24.67, V = .24, p < .001.
For Post-Tour Commitments, X^2 (6) = 32.41, V = .27, p < .001.

However, when asked about their overall need to sign out on time, both males and females responded similarly, as shown in Table 7-8. This may be due to the number of more "gender-neutral" time constraints that contributed to the need for a timely end of tour. Commuting concerns in particular may be diluting the gender-differentiated impact of family commitments, because commuting concerns are ranked highest both in post-tour frequency and correlation with sign-out need. It is also possible that female officers whose family obligations are most intractable have gravitated to the non-patrol assignments and are thus excluded from the Core Sample.

Table 7-8. *Gender and Need to for Timely End of Tour* (N = 446)							
Item 31. Overall, how often do you feel you must end your tour on time because any of the above commitments or concerns?							

Number & Percent within Gender							
	Rarely/ Never	1x–4x/ Month	1x/ Week	2x / Week	3x / Week	4x / Week	≥5x / Week	Total
Male	81 (21.4%)	61 (16.1%)	18 (4.7%)	36 (9.5%)	56 (14.8%)	38 (10.0%)	89 (23.5%)	379 (100%)
Female	16 (23.9%)	10 (14.9%)	2 (3.0%)	4 (6.0%)	7 (10.4%)	6 (9.0%)	22 (32.8%)	67 (100%)

Note. X^2 (6) = 4.22, V = .10, p > 05.

These responses show that because of personal commitments, officers often feel that they cannot extend their tour and, implicitly, cannot make any non-essential arrests. The time demands of commuting, family, social engagements, personal business, second jobs, and school (if right after work) correlate with a greater need to end the tour on time. This need for timely sign-out is significantly greater for the No-Arrest officers than for High-Arrest officers, a clear indication that sign-out need is linked to actual arrest-avoidance. However, sign-out need is not greater for women officers despite their greater family commitments. This result is consistent with the finding that females and males made the same number of arrests.

CHAPTER EIGHT

The Miseries of Arrest Processing

(Survey Items 32–34)

Arrest processing would be so much easier and more cops would probably make more arrests if the PAAs would assist us in giving us our 61 #s, Aided #s, etc. in a timely fashion, if there was an APO to give us an arrest #, and if the print machines weren't constantly breaking down, and that's just in the PD—the ADAs make you wait hours to draw up a complaint—the complainant is sometimes uncooperative and the experience in central booking is just horrible. Not to mention the condition of the perp—if the perp is sick or dirty, who wants to deal with that. However, I still DO MY JOB!!

Participant 303

Change the f-ing system... It's set up to jam you up and set you up—I would like to see less paperwork and less prisoner contact when you make an arrest.

Participant 378

We have seen that the *duration* of arrest processing affects overtime income and outside commitments, which, in turn, affect arrest behavior. We will now examine how the *duress* of processing procedures also has personal consequences that may influence arrest-making. Participants are asked to rate various unpleasant aspects of arrest processing according to how frequently each one concerns them. They are then asked how often these discomforts and risks discouraged them from making an arrest.

As described earlier, these arrest-processing concerns are of two types: those relating to administrative procedures and those relating to the handling of prisoners. The magnitude of each concern is compared through its *Concern Index* score, derived, like the previous Indexes, by multiplying each concern rating (0 = *Never*, 1 = *Rarely*, etc.) by the percentage of officers in each rating category and then adding the products. The maximum achievable Concern Index Score is 400, that is, 4 (*Always*), x 100%.

Table 8-1 displays Core Sample ratings for Administrative Concerns, ordered by their Index scores. The list reveals that the number-one fear among respondents is the "need to write lengthy or difficult narrative." For 61.4% of officers, this is often or always a concern. This may reflect the weak writing skill of many officers, and the criticism it draws from supervisors or prosecutors who review arrest paperwork.

Table 8-1. *Concerns over Administrative Procedures*
Item 32. Below are aspects of arrest-making's <u>administrative procedures</u> that may be unpleasant or risky. Please indicate the degree to which each item is a concern for <u>you</u>.

Administrative Processing Problem	N	Number and Valid Percent of Officers reporting…					Administrative Concern Index [a]
		Never a Concern	Rarely a Concern	Some-times a Concern	Often a Concern	Always a Concern	
May need to write lengthy or difficult narrative	503	24 (4.8%)	31 (6.2 %)	139 (27.6%)	175 (34.8%)	134 (26.6%)	272
May need to testify	504	43 (8.5 %)	39 (7.7 %)	120 (23.8%)	162 (32.1%)	140 (27.8%)	263
May make mistake/look bad/be reprimanded	502	49 (9.8 %)	39 (7.7 %)	109 (21.7%)	185 (36.9%)	120 (23.9%)	257
Procedures may be complex or confusing	503	29 (5.8 %)	64 (12.7%)	154 (30.6%)	154 (30.6%)	102 (20.3%)	247
May be disciplined for taking too long	502	74 (14.7%)	66 (13.1%)	115 (22.9%)	131 (26.1%)	116 (23.1%)	230
Arrest forms are boring and repetitious	503	90 (17.9%)	87 (17.3%)	110 (21.9%)	118 (23.5%)	98 (19.5%)	210
May need to go to different locations, e.g., DWI	503	89 (17.7%)	74 (14.7)%	145 (28.8%)	134 (26.6%)	61 (12.1%)	201
Procedures are tiring, especially after working eight hours	503	65 (12.9%)	88 (17.5%)	189 (37.5%)	102 (20.3%)	59 (11.7%)	200
Staff with computer/equipment skills may be unavailable	502	172 (34.3%)	147 (29.3%)	102 (20.3%)	46 (9.2 %)	35 (7.0%)	126
Computer/other processing equipment may be down	503	171 (34.0%)	154 (30.6%)	119 (23.7%)	36 (7.2%)	23 (4.6%)	118

[a] Row sum of (Percent of Officers each Frequency Category) x (Frequency of Concern). Scored from 0 (*Never*) to 4 (*Always*) Maximum possible Administrative Concern Index score is 400.

The second greatest worry is testifying in court, with 59.9% calling it often or always a concern. This is perhaps because it involves spending hours in a grimy waiting area and *then* submitting to aggressive cross-examination on the witness stand. Fear of humiliation may also explain the third highest concern, as rated by index score: that the officer may make a mistake, look bad, or be reprimanded. This is often or always on the minds of fully 60.8% of officers.

The next item, complex or confusing arrest procedures, is often or always a concern to 50.9% of officers. This may be a reaction to how frequently such procedures are amended by commanders, higher police executives, and ranking members of the prosecutor's office.

Being disciplined for taking too long follows on the list, often or always reported by 49.2% of officers. This issue is explored in later survey items, wherein most officers state that they are allowed from two to three hours for arrest processing (prisoner photos, fingerprints, medical screening, rap-sheet retrieval, and numerous arrest forms). They further report that they usually have enough time to complete the procedures, but when they exceed time limits and incur extra overtime, they are likely to be disciplined.

The next biggest complaint is that arrest forms are boring and repetitious, with 43.0% of responses in the often or always category. As noted in Chapter 1, the basic Arrest Report Worksheet required responses to over one hundred questions, even if many were not applicable. Officers must hand-write the same information on the arrest report, complaint report, medical treatment report, and often, property vouchers, requests for lab analysis, supporting depositions, and whatever additional forms the prosecutor's office requires.

Often or always, 38.7% of officers are troubled by the prospect of having to go to several locations. This situation arises when prisoners must be taken to the hospital, answer outstanding warrants from other city boroughs, or be tested for driving while intoxicated (DWI) at an outside facility. Officers face many extra hours of processing and sometimes the additional discomfort of unfamiliar locations and procedures.

Nearly the same Index score is given to concern over fatigue. Thirty-two percent of officers report that procedures are often or always tiring, especially after working eight hours. However, as discussed earlier, participants admitted making one-quarter of their arrests in the last hour of their tour (Table 4-6). Thus, they themselves bear some responsibility for their late-tour fatigue and cannot blame only the arduous arrest procedures.

The last two concerns are that staff with computer or equipment skills may be unavailable, and computers or other processing equipment may be down. As described earlier, officers often depend on civilians or in-house arrest processing officers to input arrest data and take digital photo and fingerprints. In part, this is because many officers make less than one arrest per month (Figure 4-2), so their skills grow rusty. But this dependency was also due to computer programs so antiquated and cumbersome that only a regular user could master them. Thus, when a staff member needed for arrest-processing is backlogged, out sick, on meal break, or "has an attitude," processing may be seriously delayed.

Table 8-2. *Other Concerns Regarding Administrative Procedures:*
Typical Comments

Related to Listed Concerns

Nobody knows what to do when asking something.
Too many forms compared to other agencies.
Too much repetitious paperwork— useless information.
Working in different boroughs—everything is different.
Reprimanded for mistakes with vouchers and property.
Arrest processing officer never working.
Some civilian employees are surly and obnoxious.
Equipment outdated and inoperable.
Paperwork not available, no film for camera, etc.

Critical of Supervisors

Being rushed to avoid overtime.
Overtime [requests] are scrutinized and kicked back for BS reasons.
Stress of not getting treated fair from upper ranks.
Supervisors who don't know what the hell they're doing.

Critical of Assistant District Attorneys

Everyone with a law degree wants their own form.
Having to change affidavit.
ADA dropping charge.
ADAs don't answer phone for hours.
Making an arrest around 2300 when the [ADAs go off duty] and being told to do a day
tour the next day.

Other Issues

Dirty work areas.
Lack of training.
Can't bring prisoner to Central Booking until prints clear; sometimes it takes 3 to 3.5 hrs
Feel like you're wasting (LOSING?) time away from family—perps are usually let go in a
few hours.
There shouldn't be quotas. Arrests should be made when they are in front of you, not
for the needs of the department.
The [commanding officer] likes to change charges to improve numbers so he won't look
bad at COMPSTAT and won't get yelled at by chief.

Summary Comments

I don't make collars ever.
Arrest processing is horrendous.
The whole system sucks.

To these staffing variables are added frequent mechanical problems, such as a faulty phone line, broken fax machine, shortage of toner, or downed computer link to central records. However, these human and technological delays are often or always of concern to only 16.2% and 11.8% of participants, respectively. Perhaps this is because such problems augment officers' arrest overtime without subjecting them to blame from supervisors.

Officers are also asked to describe any other administrative problems, and 140 of the 506 participants responded. Table 8-2 quotes some typical comments.

Item 33 asks officers about prisoner-related problems in arrest processing. Like Table 8-1, Table 8-3 orders Core Sample responses by Index score, calculated in the same manner as are administrative problems.

Table 8-3. *Concerns over Prisoner-Related Problems*

Item 33. Below are aspects of handling arrested persons that may be unpleasant or risky. Please indicate the degree to which each item is a concern for you.

Prisoner-Related Problem	N	Number and Valid Percent of Officers Reporting					
		Never a Concern	*Rarely* a Concern	*Sometimes* a Concern	*Often* a Concern	*Always* a Concern	Prisoner Concern Index[a]
Prisoner may be verbally abusive.	505	30 (5.9 %)	54 (10.7%)	132 (26.1%)	159 (31.5%)	130 (25.7%)	260
Prisoner may make allegations (CCRB, IAB, etc.)	503	104 (20.7%)	61 (12.1%)	112 (22.3%)	137 (27.2%)	89 (17.7%)	209
Prisoner may be EDP/Drunk.	504	43 (8.5 %)	85 (16.9%)	228 (45.2%)	109 (21.6%)	39 (7.7%)	203
Prisoner may be violent.	505	86 (16.9%)	69 (13.7%)	232 (45.9%)	81 (16.0%)	37 (7.3%)	183
Prisoner may try to escape.	503	158 (31.4%)	48 (9.3 %)	90 (17.9%)	145 (28.8%)	62 (12.3%)	181
Prisoner may need to go to hospital.	503	87 (17.3%)	113 (22.5%)	197 (39.2%)	80 (15.9%)	26 (5.2%)	169
Prisoner may be filthy, have foul odor.	502	116 (23.1%)	151 (30.1%)	158 (31.5%)	57 (11.4%)	20 (4.0%)	143
Prisoner may be infectious (AIDS, TB, lice, etc.).	505	231 (45.7%)	117 (23.2%)	122 (24.2%)	24 (4.8%)	11 (2.2%)	94

[a] Row sum of (Percent of Officers each Frequency Category) x (Frequency of Concern). Frequency of Concern scored from 0 (*Never*) to 4 (*Always*) Maximum possible Index score is 400.

Despite their thick-skinned public image, officers rate verbal abuse by prisoners as their most common concern. This might be explained by the fact that prisoners cannot be left unattended and sometimes berate offi-cers relentlessly through every step of processing. Often, their requests for a phone call, a bathroom, a cigarette, or a dose of methadone—if not granted immediately—are followed by a stream of epithets. This behavior often or always bothers as much as 57.2% of officers.

The second most frequent worry is that the prisoner may make allega-tions to the Internal Affairs Bureau or the Civilian Complaint Review Board. For 44.9% of participants, there is often or always a possibility that a prisoner will accuse them of stealing their property or abusing them physically or verbally. The high rating reflects the potential career damage inflicted by such accusations. Under department policy, supervisors must report all allegations to the Internal Affairs Bureau (IAB) and/or Civilian Complaint Review Board (CCRB), or put their own careers in jeopardy.

Nearly as widespread a problem are prisoners who may be drunk or emotionally disturbed. For 29.3% of respondents, this is often or always a concern. This may reflect the high proportion of arrestees who are agi-tated or ill from substance abuse or who are mentally ill and without their prescribed medications. The officer must move such prisoners through arrest processing using minimal force, though they may be incoherent, uncooperative, or belligerent.

A related fear is that the prisoner may be violent. Some 23.3% of par-ticipants often or always feel endangered by their prisoners. Many arrest procedures require the unarmed officer to be in close physical contact with the uncuffed detainee. But officer injury is not the only negative con-sequence of a violent outburst. If the prisoner is hurt, he or she must be taken to the hospital. Moreover, IAB and CCRB must be notified and may conduct an investigation.

The chance that the prisoner may try to escape is often or always a concern of 41.1% of respondents. This is higher than might be expected, given the rarity of escapes compared to the other listed prisoner-related concerns. The explanation may be that these incidents often receive em-barrassing media attention and are punished more severely than most other infractions.

Taking a prisoner to the hospital is often or always a concern for 21.1% officers. Such trips are common among arrestees for a host of rea-sons: injuries received during their crime or arrest, detoxification from alcohol or drugs, psychiatric examination, treatment for previous ailments like AIDS or gangrene, replacement doses of routine medication, or some-times fabricated complaints. Officers must wait with their prisoners in non-secured emergency rooms, often for many hours, before returning to their commands to resume processing.

Prisoners who may be filthy or have a foul odor are often or always a concern to 15.4% of respondents. Such prisoners are often homeless, and in an enclosed patrol car or arrest processing room, their physical condition may actually nauseate the officer. The probable reason officers ranked this as a lower concern is that they do not arrest such individuals unless they feel they have no choice.

The least concern is the possibility that the prisoner may have an infectious disease; only 7.0% of officers often or always consider this danger. This may indicate an increased understanding of how HIV and AIDS are transmitted as well as a wider availability of protective gloves and masks.

Forty-five officers described other prisoner-related concerns. Some typical comments are quoted in Table 8-4.

Table 8-4. *Other Concerns Regarding the Handling of Prisoner: Typical Comments*
Related to Listed Concerns
Accusations of racial profiling. *CCRB makes it possible for lawbreakers to retaliate against cops.* *Prisoner suing officer.* *Possibility of getting hurt.* *EDPs at psycho ward; hospital connections should take them off our hands.* *Arresting officer so busy with paperwork that it is impossible to watch prisoner.* *Homeless prisoner using cell as bathroom.* *Prisoner injured, handicapped, filthy.* *Prisoner spitting at you, trying to bite.*
Other Prisoner Issues
May have fingers not conducive to fingerprint machine. *Prisoners uncooperative—refuse info/prints.* *Speaks foreign language only.* *Prisoner who knows people on the Job.* *Deception.* *Prisoner has to pee every 5 minutes.*
Critical of Shortages
Improper cells (lack of) for males/females. *Not enough cell area for prisoners.* *Lack of in-house equipment (non-lethal-straps/tasers).*
Critical of Supervisors
Boss angry at you for bringing in a skell [derelict] even when you have no choice. *Supervisors afraid to use [non-lethal] devices for fear of liability.* *Supervisors may be intimidated by complaining prisoner and order voided arrest.*
Fear of Mishap and Its Disciplinary Consequences
What would happen if prisoner hung himself while A/O is busy with paperwork? *Razor blade hidden under tongue of shoe, found at Central Booking.* *Property and prisoners—Best way to get jammed up.*

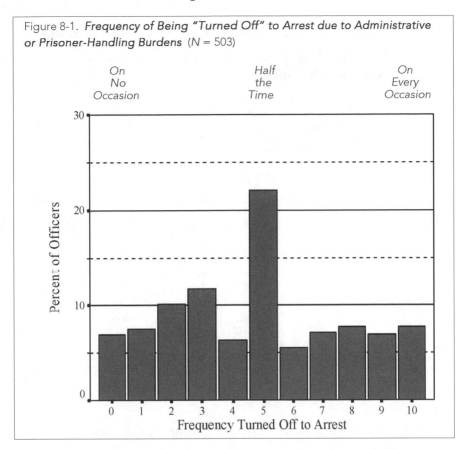

Figure 8-1. *Frequency of Being "Turned Off" to Arrest due to Administrative or Prisoner-Handling Burdens* (N = 503)

The final item in this section (see Figure 8-1) asks how often the Core Sample officers are actually "turned off" from making arrests as a result of administrative and prisoner-handling concerns. On a scale from 0 (*On no occasion*) to 10 (*On every occasion*), officers' mean score is 4.8, or nearly "half the time" ($SD = 2.9$).

The No-Arrest Group gave a mean rating of 5.7 ($SD = 3.0$, $n = 151$), significantly higher than the High-Arrest Group's mean rating of 3.5 ($SD = 2.4$, $n = 151$). Thus, the non-arresting officers found arrest processing to be considerably more of a "turn-off" than those officers making three or more arrests per month; $t (224.596) = 5.994$, $p < .001$.

Officers who report more frequent and numerous concerns over the hardships of arrest processing also report greater distaste toward making an arrest. Tables 8-5 and 8-6 respectively list administrative and prisoner-handling problems, ordered by their degree of correlation to arrest aversion, or being "turned off" to arrest. They show significant relationships ($p < .001$) between aversion and both types of concerns.

Table 8-5. *Correlation between Administrative Processing Concerns and Aversion to Arrest-Making*

Administrative Processing Problem	r_s	N
Procedures are tiring, especially after working eight hrs.	.50***	501
Arrest forms are boring and repetitious	.44***	500
May be disciplined for taking too long	.41***	500
Procedures may be complex or confusing	.39***	501
Staff w. computer/equipment skills may be unavailable	.38***	500
May make mistake/ look bad / be reprimanded	.38***	500
May need to testify	.35***	502
May need to write lengthy or difficult narrative	.35***	501
May need to go to different locations, e.g., DWI.	.35***	501
Computer/other processing equipment may be down	.31***	501
All Administrative Processing Problems[a]	.58***	491

a Sum of participants' ratings for each prisoner problem, correlated with arrest making aversion.
***Correlation is significant to .001 level (2-tailed).

Table 8-6. *Correlation between Prisoner-Handling Problems and Aversion to Arrest-Making*

Prisoner-Related Problem	r_s	N
Prisoner may make allegations (CCRB, IAB, etc.).	.32***	501
Prisoner may need to go to hospital.	.31***	501
Prisoner may be filthy, have foul odor.	.29***	501
Prisoner may be EDP/Drunk.	.26***	503
Prisoner may be violent.	.24***	503
Prisoner may be verbally abusive.	.18***	503
Prisoner may be infectious (AIDS, TB, lice, etc.)	.18***	503
Prisoner may try to escape.	.15***	501
All Prisoner-Related Problems[a]	.33***	497

a Sum of participants' ratings for each prisoner problem, correlated with arrest-making aversion
***Correlation is significant to .001 level (2-tailed).

The last row of each table correlates, respectively, each participant's total ratings for administrative and prisoner concerns with his or her score for arrest aversion. They show that overall, administrative concerns are more highly associated with arrest aversion (r_s = .58) than are prisoner concerns (r_s = .33). Moreover, *every* administrative problem except equipment breakdowns is more closely linked to arrest "turn-off" than *any* unpleasant aspect of handling prisoners. This finding conforms to a view expressed by officers throughout my police career: "The perps I can handle. It's the bosses you have to watch out for."

It is also notable that the concerns that best predict arrest-avoidance are not necessarily the ones deemed most common (see Tables 8-1 and 8-3). For instance, writing a lengthy or difficult narrative is rated the most frequent administrative concern, but the fatigue associated with lengthy procedures is the factor most related to arrest aversion. Similarly, verbal abuse is deemed the most common prisoner-handling concern, but prisoner allegations are rated highest as an arrest deterrent.

We see then that the arrest-processing ordeal not only thwarts personal plans, but also evokes strongly negative personal feelings. Officers' most frequent administrative concerns all involve a fear of being humiliated: having to write a narrative, having to testify in court, and making a mistake, looking bad, or being reprimanded. Officers' most frequent prisoner-handling concerns are not the varied physical dangers but the verbal ones: being incessantly berated or accused of misconduct subject to a departmental investigation.

Because of arrest processing difficulties, officers are "turned off" to arrest processing nearly half the time. For every listed aspect of the ordeal, officers who report more concern also report a greater aversion to arrest processing. And, in keeping with the comments of police colleagues, the officers worry more about the bosses than the prisoners: Overall, arrest aversion is more highly associated with administrative problems than with prisoner-handling problems.

The evidence that being "turned off" to arrest processing is linked to actual arrest avoidance again comes from the comparison of No-Arrest and High-Arrest officers. We find the No-Arresters' aversion-to-processing scores are substantially greater than those of the High-Arrest group.

CHAPTER NINE

Arrest-Control Adaptations

(Survey Items 35–39)

Our findings so far indicate that overtime need, time constraints, and arrest-processing burdens provide personal motives to seek and shun arrests. Yet to be established is whether officers have the *means* to control their arrest-making.

ARREST-SEEKING ADAPTATIONS

The participants were presented with a list of 14 strategies to increase arrest overtime, and asked how frequently they use each one. Their responses are listed in Table 9-1, ordered by scores in the *Arrest-Seeking Index*. These are derived, as are previous index scores, by multiplying each rating (0 = *Never*, 1 = *Rarely*, etc.) by the percentage of officers in each rating category and then adding the products. The maximum possible Index score is 400.

Table 9-1 shows that participants use every overtime-seeking adaptation presented. Yet few officers—between 13.4% and 2.0%—apply any one overtime-seeking technique *often* or *always*. The low percentages in these categories probably reflect the generally low arrest rates among participants and the large choice of arrest-seeking strategies available.

The responses suggest that officers patrol differently in the second half of their tour, when they are "looking" (i.e., arrest-seeking). Conversely, when officers are early in their tour and *not* looking, they may not be at their crime-fighting best. They might *not* rush to crime scenes, patrol on easy-arrest blocks, or perform license-plate checks or investigatory stops, or try hard to find suspects, or engage in other self-directed enforcement activities.

The most questionable arrest-seeking tactics are the least common. Sometimes, often, or always, 11.5% of officers try to handle jobs before alerting the dispatcher, allowing them to turn an incident into an arrest situation before a supervisor or other officers could influence the outcome. At least sometimes, 7.8% of officers issue a Desk Appearance Ticket instead of a summons, so that a minor offender who ordinarily would be briefly detained at the scene is instead arrested and held for six or more hours. And, at least sometimes, 5.6% focus more on minority individuals who might be perps, a practice akin to racial profiling.

Table 9-1. *Methods of Arrest-Seeking for Overtime*

Item 35. *Below are methods officers might use to increase their arrest overtime. Please indicate the extent to which you may have used each method for the purpose of increasing arrest overtime.*

| Method | N | Number and Valid Percent of Officers Who Report Using Method... | | | | | Arrest-Seeking Index[a] |
		Never	Rarely	Some-times	Often	Always	
Tried to arrive faster at crimes in progress in 2nd half of tour	500	167 (33.4%)	143 (28.6%)	123 (24.6%)	53 (10.6%)	14 (2.8%)	121
Patrolled in areas known for easy arrests in 2nd half of tour	502	178 (35.5%)	121 (24.1%)	148 (29.5%)	41 (8.2%)	14 (2.8%)	119
Tried hard to find suspects who left scene in 2nd half of tour	500	184 (36.8%)	132 (26.4%)	132 (26.4%)	45 (9.0%)	7 (1.4%)	112
Made more mobile computer checks and/or car stops in 2nd half of tour	501	183 (36.5%)	148 (29.5%)	116 (23.3%)	41 (8.2%)	13 (2.6%)	111
Asked officers for their unwanted arrests	502	191 (38.0%)	152 (30.3%)	127 (25.3%)	24 (4.8%)	8 (1.6%)	102
Tried to take domestic incident jobs in 2nd half of tour	500	202 (40.4%)	156 (31.2%)	104 (20.8%)	32 (6.4%)	6 (1.2%)	97
Switched to assignment with good arrest opportunities	501	229 (45.7%)	148 (29.5%)	88 (17.6%)	26 (5.2%)	10 (2.0%)	88
Tried harder to get complainants to prosecute in 2nd half of tour	497	244 (49.1%)	162 (32.6%)	64 (12.8%)	20 (4.0%)	7 (1.4%)	76
Looked for any minor violation in 2nd half of tour	502	251 (50.0%)	159 (31.7%)	70 (13.9%)	14 (2.8%)	8 (1.6%)	74
Made more Stop/Question/Frisks in 2nd half of tour	502	252 (50.2%)	168 (33.5%)	61 (12.2%)	19 (3.8%)	2 (0.4%)	71
Followed up on every pick-up complaint[b] in 2nd half of tour	502	256 (51.0%)	164 (32.7%)	67 (13.3%)	13 (2.6%)	2 (0.4%)	69
Tried to handle jobs before telling dispatcher in 2nd half of tour	496	277 (55.8%)	162 (32.7%)	42 (8.5%)	11 (2.2%)	4 (0.8%)	60
Issued a DAT instead of a summons in 2nd half of tour	501	350 (69.9%)	112 (22.4%)	29 (5.8%)	5 (1.0%)	5 (1.0%)	41
Focused more on minority individuals who might be perps	500	384 (76.8%)	88 (17.6%)	18 (3.6%)	5 (1.0%)	5 (1.0%)	32

[a] Row sum of (Percent of Officers in each frequency category) x (Frequency of Use) Frequency of use categories scored from 0 (*Never*) to 4 (*Always*). Maximum Index Score is 400.
[b] A pick-up complaint is one that the officer happens upon while patrolling, rather than one that is assigned.

Officers then describe other methods they use to increase arrest overtime. Some offer additional tactics to catch an offender, such as "Follow the crack heads and junkies," "Patrol areas not normally covered," "Hide and wait for someone to jump turnstile," and "Focus on repeat offenders." However, others revealed ways to "milk the arrest" (i.e., extend processing overtime) such as "Take my sweet time & dot every i and cross every t," "Use Supporting Deposition arrests and slows process," and "Have complainant come in at a later time to process arrest at precinct."

Next, the survey asks officers how often they use *any* overtime-seeking arrest techniques. As Table 9-2 shows, the officers who deploy such measures at least once per week add up to only 17.9% of participants. This somewhat infrequent arrest-seeking is consistent with officers' infrequent arrest-making.

Table 9-2. *Overall Use of Arrest-Seeking Measures for Overtime*
Item 36. How often overall do you take measures like those in Table 9-1 to make arrests because you need overtime money?

Number and Valid Percent of Officers							
Never/ Rarely	1–4x/ Month	1x/ Week	2x/ Week	3x/ Week	4x/ Week	5x/ week	Total
307 (61.9%)	100 (20.2%)	34 (6.9%)	30 (6.0%)	16 (3.2%)	4 (.08%)	5 (1.0%)	496 (100%)

However, those in the No-Arrest Group use arrest overtime-seeking tactics substantially less than Core Sample, while those in the High-Arrest Group use such tactics substantially more, as Table 9-3 illustrates. For instance, 10.8% of No-Arrest officers, as compared to 34.4% of High-Arrest officers use these measures at least once a week.

Table 9-3. *Overall Frequency of Arrest-Seeking Measures aimed at Increasing Overtime for No-Arrest and High-Arrest Officers*
Item 36. How often overall do you take measures like those in Table 9-1 to make arrests because you need overtime money?

	Number and Valid Percent within No-Arrest and High-Arrest Groups						
	Rarely/ Never	1x–4x / month	1x / Week	2x / Week	3x / Week	4x-5x / Week	Total
No-Arrest	113 (76.4%)	19 (12.8%)	8 (5.4%)	4 (2.7%)	3 (2.0%)	1 (.7%)	148 (100%)
High-Arrest	40 (44.4%)	19 (21.1%)	10 (11.1%)	11 (12.2%)	6 (6.7%)	4 (4.4%)	90 (100%)

Note. X^2 (5) = 28.69, p < .001.

In Chapter 6, we saw that High-Arrest officers report a greater need for arrest overtime, and that the entire Core Sample's overtime need scores cluster at midrange and at the maximum (see Figure 6-4). When this arrest overtime need is correlated with officers' overall overtime-seeking behaviors, we find a significant relationship: $r_s = .39$, $p < .001$, $N = 489$. That is, officers who report a greater need for arrest overtime money also report more frequent use of arrest-seeking adaptations aimed at making overtime.

Women officers, because of their greater family commitments, might be expected to use arrest overtime-seeking measures less often. The ratings seem to support this, but do not reach statistical significance, as shown in Table 9-4. This conforms to the earlier findings that Core Sample women and men are alike in both their rates of arrest and their overall sign-out need.

Table 9-4. *Overall Frequency of Arrest-Seeking Measures aimed at Increasing Overtime for Male and Female Officers* (N=442)

Item 36. How often overall do you take measures like those in Table 9-1 to make arrests because you need overtime money?

	Frequency and Percent within Gender				
	Rarely/Never	1x–4x / month	1x /Week	2x–5x/Week	Total
Males	220 (58.8%)	81 (21.7%)	24 (6.4%)	49 (13.1%)	374 (100%)
Females	47 (69.1%)	13 (19.1%)	5 (7.4%)	3 (4.4%)	68 (100%)

Note. $X^2 (3) = 4.95$, $p > .05$.

Officers who work the midnight shift also respond contrary to an expectation. Their arrests are potentially the most lucrative (because, as explained in Chapter 1, they cannot be rescheduled to "straight time"), and any questionable arrest-seeking tactics are less likely to be observed by supervisors or law-abiding citizens. Nevertheless, as Table 9-5 indicates, midnight shift officers do *not* engage in more arrest-generating adaptations than their day-tour and evening-tour colleagues. This is in keeping with the earlier finding that the arrest rates of the three tours are statistically equal.

Table 9-5. *Overall Frequency of Arrest-Seeking Measures Aimed at Increasing Overtime for Officers on Midnight, Day, and Evening Tours* (N=424)

Item 36. How often overall do you take measures like those in Table 9-1 to make arrests because you need overtime money?

	Frequency and Percent within Tour					
	Rarely/ Never	1–4 x / Month	1x / Week	2x / Week	3x–5x / Week	Total
Midnights	50 (56.8%)	22 (25.0%)	7 (8.0%)	4 (4.5%)	5 (5.7%)	88 (100%)
Days	110 (65.5%)	31 (18.5%)	9 (5.4%)	9 (5.4%)	9 (5.4%)	168 (100%)
Evenings	106 (63.1%)	36 (21.4%)	11 (6.5%)	7 (4.2%)	8 (4.8%)	168 (100%)

Note. $X^2 (8) = 2.90$, $V = .58$, $p > .05$.

Officers from the borough of the Bronx have the highest arrest rates, 2.1 per month, and the longest processing time, 10.48 hours. At the other extreme are officers from Queens, who make 1.2 arrests per month and have a processing time of 8.10 hours. Because Bronx officers are the most accustomed to arrest-making, arrest-processing, and arrest overtime money, they would be expected to use arrest-seeking tactics significantly more than their Queens counterparts. Table 9-6 confirms this pattern; we see, for instance, that 22.1% of Bronx officers as opposed to 18.5% of Queens officers report taking measures to increase arrest overtime at least once per week. The borough disparities are statistically significant.

Table 9-6. *Overall Frequency of Arrest-Seeking Measures aimed at Increasing Overtime for Officers from the Bronx and Queens* (n=180)

Item 36. How often overall do you take measures like those in Table 9-1 to make arrests because you need overtime money?

	Frequency and Valid Percent within Borough					
	Rarely / Never	1–4 x / Month	1x / Week	2x / Week	3x–5x / Week	Total
Borough of the Bronx	42 (54.5%)	18 (23.4%)	3 (3.9%)	10 (13.0%)	4 (5.2%)	77 (100%)
Borough of Queens	65 (63.1%)	19 (18.4%)	11 (10.7%)	2 (1.9%)	6 (5.8%)	103 (100%)

Note. $X^2 (4) = 11.77$, $V = .26$, $p = .019$.

ARREST-AVOIDANCE ADAPTATIONS

The survey next presents a list of 12 arrest-avoidance strategies aimed at leaving work on time and/or escaping the burdens of arrest processing, again asking officers how often they use each one. Table 9-7 lists each method, ordered by scores in the *Arrest-Avoidance Index*. As with arrest seeking, the Index scores are derived by multiplying each rating (0 = *Never*, 1 = *Rarely*, etc.) by the percentage of officers in each rating category and then adding the products. The maximum possible Index score is 400.

Table 9-7. **Methods of Avoiding Arrest**
Item 37. Below are methods officers might use to avoid making arrests. Please indicate the extent to which you may have used each method in order to get off work on time, and/or avoid the discomforts and risks of arrest processing.

Method	N	Number and Valid Percent of Officers Who Report Using Method...					Arrest Avoidance Index[a]
		Never	Rarely	Sometimes	Often	Always	
Conducted few or no Stop / Question / Frisks	498	124 (24.9%)	119 (23.9%)	120 (24.1%)	77 (15.5%)	58 (11.6%)	165
Made few or no RMP computer checks / car stops	499	112 (22.4%)	123 (24.6%)	154 (30.9%)	75 (15.0%)	35 (7.0%)	159
Ignored minor violations (e.g., drinking/ urinating/ smoking weed)	501	153 (30.5%)	136 (27.1%)	136 (27.1%)	53 (10.6%)	23 (4.6%)	135
Avoided patrol areas where arrests "fall into your lap"	495	163 (32.9%)	122 (24.6%)	112 (22.6%)	72 (14.3%)	27 (5.6%)	135
Asked fellow officers to take any arrest you may get stuck with	499	136 (27.3%)	137 (27.5%)	164 (32.9%)	48 (9.6%)	14 (2.8%)	133
Arranged to get assignment having little or no chance to arrest	498	175 (35.1%)	133 (26.7%)	131 (26.3%)	45 (9.0%)	14 (2.8%)	118
Issued a summons instead of making an arrest	500	175 (35.0%)	145 (29.4%)	133 (26.6%)	32 (6.4%)	13 (2.6%)	112
Drove slowly or conspicuously (lights, sirens) to crimes in progress	500	235 (47.0%)	130 (26.0%)	76 (15.2%)	36 (7.2%)	23 (4.6%)	96
Ignored pick-up complaints from non-involved parties	499	221 (44.3%)	152 (30.5%)	82 (16.4%)	28 (5.6%)	16 (3.2%)	93
Tried to discourage complainants from pressing charges	500	263 (52.6%)	124 (24.8%)	85 (17.0%)	19 (3.8%)	9 (1.8%)	77
Avoided assignments to domestic incidents	499	260 (52.1%)	139 (27.9%)	67 (13.4%)	21 (4.2%)	12 (2.4%)	77
Tried to dispose of jobs without alerting dispatcher/supervisor	496	281 (56.7%)	119 (24.0%)	67 (13.5%)	15 (3.0%)	14 (2.8%)	71

[a] Row sum of (percent of officers in each frequency category) x (frequency of use). Frequency of use categories scored from 0 (*Never*) to 4 (*Always*). Maximum possible Index Score is 400.

Officers use all of the listed arrest-avoidance methods. Between 27.1% and 5.8% of officers use any single avoidance tactic *often* or *always*. The most popular strategies involve refraining from such self-initiated actions as conducting stop-and-frisks, patrolling easy-arrest blocks, confronting "quality-of-life" offenders, or investigating motorists. Less frequently applied are the more questionable tactics, such as trying to arrive at a crime scene *after* the suspect has fled, ignoring a tip from a "concerned citizen," and dissuading a victim from pressing charges.

Officers then describe other ways they evade arrest-making. One approach is to simply stay off patrol, for example, "Become a house mouse," "Take the day [off]," "Stay on TS (telephone switchboard)," and "Park." Another tactic was to stay busy with other activities, such as "Take a lot of 62Ps and 62As" (bathroom breaks and administrative errands), "Get a Row Tow" (find a stolen auto requiring prolonged processing), and "Hold on to job until EOT" (end of tour). And, if an arrest situation does arise, deception may be necessary: "Convince complainant that incident is not really a crime" or "Lied to victim about possible charges or seriousness of crime."

The next two survey items ask how often per month or week officers use arrest-avoidance techniques, either to get off work on time or to avoid the burdens of arrest processing. Table 9-8 indicates that as a reason to avoid arrest, sign-out need outweighs processing concerns. For instance, at least once a week, 33.9% are influenced by the need for timely sign-out, and 25.3% are influenced by the burdens of processing.

Table 9-8.*Overall Use of Arrest-Avoidance Measures*

Items 38–39. How often overall do you take measures to avoid arrests like those in Table 9-7...
...because you need to get off work on time?
...because of risks/discomforts of administrative procedures or handling prisoners?

Reason for Avoiding Arrest	Number and Valid Percent of Officers							
	Never/ Rarely	1–4x/ Month	1x/ Week	2x/ Week	3x/ Week	4x/ Week	5x/ Week	Total
Get Off Work on Time	226 (45.3%)	104 (20.8%)	33 (6.6%)	38 (7.6%)	37 (7.4%)	21 (4.2%)	40 (8.0%)	449 (100%)
Processing Risks/ Discomforts	283 (56.8%)	89 (17.9%)	17 (3.4%)	32 (6.4%)	20 (4.0%)	21 (4.2%)	36 (7.2%)	448 (100%)

Of course, both time pressures and processing burdens may simultaneously discourage officers from making arrests. The two factors prove to be highly correlated: $r_s = .67$, $p < .001$, $N = 498$.

The No-Arrest Group uses arrest-avoidance techniques significantly more often than the High-Arrest Group, as shown in Table 9-9. For instance, in order to sign out on time, 40.3% of No-Arrest officers versus

21.6% of the High-Arrest officers utilize avoidance measures at least once per week. Because of arrest processing concerns, 28.9% of No-Arrest officers, compared to 9.7% of High-Arrest officers, use avoidance measures within this time frame.

Table 9-9. *Overall Frequency of Arrest-Avoidance Measures for No-Arrest and High-Arrest Officers* (n = 242)

Item 38. How often overall do you take measures to avoid arrest like those in Table 9-7 because you need to get off work on time?

Officer Group	Number and Valid Percent Avoiding Arrest for Timely Sign-out				
	Rarely / Never	1x–4x / Month	1x–2x/ Week	3x–5x/ Week	Total
No-Arrest	67 (45.0%)	22 (14.8%)	17 (11.4%)	43 (28.9%)	149 (100%)
High-Arrest	46 (49.5%)	26 (28.0%)	20 (21.5%)	1 (1.1%)	93 (100%)

Item 39. How often overall do you take measures to avoid arrests like those in Table 9-7 because of the risks discomforts of administrative procedures or prisoner handling?

Officer Group	Number and Valid Percent Avoiding Arrest for Processing Concerns				
	Rarely / Never	1x–4x / Month	1x–2x / Week	3x–5x/ Week	Total
No-Arrest	84 (56.4%)	22 (14.8%)	8 (5.4%)	35 (23.5%)	149 (100%)
High-Arrest	65 (69.9%)	19 (20.4%)	7 (7.5%)	2 (2.2%)	93 (100%)

Note. For timely sign-out, $X^2 (3) = 33.40$, $V = .37$, $p < .001$.
For processing concerns, $X^2 (3) = 20.27$, $V = .29$, $p < .001$.

In the *Note* in Table 9-9, the dissimilar values for Cramer's V (.37 for sign-out concerns versus .29 for processing concerns) tell us that the No-Arrest and High-Arrest groups are more alike in their desire to get off work on time than in their feelings toward arrest processing. Perhaps this is because those officers who frequently process arrest grow more competent and comfortable with the procedures, while those who rarely arrest are deprived of the opportunity to improve.

Earlier, Tables 7-1 and 7-2 displayed officers' need to end their tours on time because of outside commitments and concerns. This need to leave work proves to be significantly related to the use of arrest-avoidance adaptations aimed at timely sign-out, shown in Table 9-8: $r_s = .30$, $p < .001$, *N*=499. Similarly, Figure 8-1 displayed how often participants are "turned off" to arrest-making due to administrative or prisoner-handling burdens. These sentiments are significantly correlated with the use of arrest-avoidance measures stemming from processing concerns shown in the lower half of Table 9-8: r_s=.56, p < .001, N=498. Stated another way, the greater an officer's eagerness to get off work on time or escape the ordeal of arrest processing, the greater will be his or her use of arrest-evading tactics.

It might be predicted that because women officers may shoulder more family-related responsibilities, they would be more likely than male officers to use arrest-avoidance methods to assure a timely end of tour. Table 9-10 rebuts this, showing statistically similar rates in the use of arrest avoidance adaptations for sign-out between males and females. This conforms to the earlier findings that Core Sample women are comparable to men in both their rates of arrest and overall sign-out need.

Table 9-10. *Overall Frequency of Arrest-Avoiding Measures aimed at Timely Sign-Out for Male and Female Officers* (N = 447)

Item 38. *How often overall do you take measures like those in Table 9-7 to avoid arrests because you need to get off work on time?*

Officer Group	Number and Valid Percent within Gender							
	Rarely/ Never	1x–4x / Month	1x / Week	2x / Week	3x / Week	4x / Week	5x / Week	Total
Males	158 (41.7%)	82 (21.6%)	27 (71.1%)	33 (8.7%)	31 (8.2%)	20 (5.3%)	28 (7.4%)	379 (100%)
Females	38 (55.9%)	15 (22.1%)	4 (5.9%)	1 (1.5%)	4 (5.9%)	0 (0%)	6 (8.8%)	68 (100%)

Note. X^2 (6) = 10.89, V = .16, p >.05.

Similarly, midnight, day, and evening tour officers in Table 9-11 show no significant differences in rates of arrest-avoiding measures for either timely sign-out or processing aversion. As with arrest-seeking (Table 9-5), the midnight officers' opportunity to earn greater arrest overtime and work more anonymously does not appear to affect the use of avoidance behaviors. This result corresponds with the similar arrest rates among the three tours.

Table 9-11. *Overall Frequency of Arrest-Avoidance Measures due to Sign-Out Need and Aversion to Processing on Midnight, Day, and Evening Tours*

Item 38. How often overall do you take measures like those in Table 9-7 to avoid arrests because you need to get off work on time?

Officer Group	Number and Valid Percent within Tour							
	Rarely/ Never	1–4 x / Month	1x / Week	2x / Week	3x / Week	4x / Week	5x / Week	Total
Midnights	33 (37.9%)	19 (21.8%)	8 (9.2%)	9 (10.3%)	6 (6.9%)	2 (2.3%)	10 (11.5%)	87 (100%)
Days	69 (40.8%)	38 (33.5%)	9 (5.3%)	16 (9.5%)	15 (8.9%)	7 (4.1%)	15 (8.9%)	169 (100%)
Evenings	86 (50.9%)	34 (20.1%)	12 (7.1%)	8 (4.7%)	11 (6.5%)	9 (5.3%)	9 (5.3%)	169 (100%)

Item 39. How often overall do you take measures like those in Table 9-7 to avoid arrests because of the risks / discomforts of administrative procedures or handling prisoners?

Officer Group	Number and Valid Percent within Tour							
	Rarely/ Never	1–4 x / Month	1x / Week	2x / Week	3x–5x / Week	2x / Week	2x / Week	Total
Midnights	47 (54.0%)	21 (24.1%)	1 (1.1%)	4 (4.6%)	2 (2.3%)	6 (6.9%)	6 (6.9%)	87 (100%)
Days	87 (51.8%)	30 (17.9%)	4 (2.4%)	16 (9.5%)	8 (4.8%)	6 (3.6%)	17 (10.1%)	168 (100%)
Evenings	103 (60.9%)	29 (17.2%)	7 (4.1%)	6 (3.6%)	8 (4.7%)	8 (4.7%)	8 (4.7%)	169 (100%)

Note. For timely sign-out, X^2 (425. 12) = 12.75, V = .17, p > .05. For processing concerns, X^2 (424.12) = 15.99, V = .14, p > .05.

Regarding borough differences, we have seen (Table 9-6) that Bronx officers employ arrest overtime-seeking tactics more often than Queens officers. Still, it is possible that the Bronx's protracted arrest procedures (2.6 hours longer than in Queens) also lead to greater use of arrest-avoidance adaptations. However, as shown in Table 9-12, Bronx and Queens officers are statistically similar in their use of arrest-avoidance measures, both for timely sign-out and processing aversion. Possibly, the markedly higher crime rates confronting Bronx officers create a basic arrest-making mindset, leading to the higher rate of arrests and consequent focus on maximizing overtime. This would offset the seemingly high incentives to avoid arrests in the Bronx.

Table 9-12. *Overall Frequency of Arrest-Avoidance Measures due to Sign-Out Need and Processing Aversion for Officers from the Bronx and Queens (n=180)*

Frequency and Valid Percent within Borough				

Item 38. *How often overall do you take measures like those in Table 9-7 to avoid arrests because you need to get off work on time?*

	Rarely / Never	1x /Month –1x Week	2–3x / Week	4–5x Week	Total
Borough of the Bronx	35 (19.4%)	19 (10.6%)	13 (7.2%)	10 (5.6%)	77 (100%)
Borough of Queens	42 (23.3%)	32 (17.8%)	18 (10.0%)	11 (6.1%)	103 (100%)

Item 39. *How often overall do you take measures like those in Table 9-7 to avoid arrests because of the risk /discomforts of administrative procedures or handling prisoners?*

	Rarely / Never	1x /Month –1x Week	2–3x / Week	4–5x Week	Total
Borough of the Bronx	44 (24.6%)	13 (7.3%)	9 (5.0%)	10 (5.6%)	77 (100%)
Borough of Queens	50 (27.9%)	31 (17.3%)	10 (5.6%)	12 (6.7%)	103 (100%)

Note. For timely sign-out, $X^2(3) = 1.071$ (3) V=.077, $p > .05$. For processing aversion, X^2 (3) = 3.999, V = .149, $p > .05$.

RELATIONSHIP OF ARREST-SEEKING AND ARREST-AVOIDANCE

Table 9-13 matches up comparable seeking and avoiding methods and their respective Index scores. While not amenable to statistical testing, the scores strongly suggest that avoidance is far more common. It outweighs the complementary seeking behavior in 10 of the 12 pairings, the exceptions being officers' reactions to crimes in progress and domestic incidents.

Arrest-avoidance also surpasses arrest-seeking when comparing overall ratings (see Tables 9-2 and 9-8). At least once a week, for instance, 17.9% of participants used arrest-seeking methods aimed at overtime, while 33.8% used avoidance tactics aimed at timely sign-out and 25.2 used avoidance tactics because of processing burdens.

Table 9-13. *Comparison of Index Scores for Arrest-Seeking and Arrest-Avoidance Measures*

Method	Seeking/ Avoidance Index Scores
Made more Stop-Question-Frisks in 2nd half of tour	71
Conducted few or no Stop-Question-Frisks	*165*
Made more MDT checks and/or car stops in 2nd half of tour	111
Made few or no RMP computer checks / car stops	*159*
Looked for any minor violation in 2nd half of tour	74
Ignored minor violations (e.g., drinking/urinating/smoking weed)	*135*
Patrolled in areas known for easy arrests in 2nd half of tour	119
Avoided patrol areas where arrests "fall into your lap"	*135*
Asked officers for their unwanted arrests	102
Asked fellow officers to take any arrest you may get stuck with	*133*
Switched to assignment with good arrest opportunities	88
Arranged to get assignment having little or no chance to arrest	*118*
Issued a DAT instead of a summons in 2nd half of tour	41
Issued a summons instead of making an arrest	*112*
Tried to arrive faster at crimes in progress in 2nd half of tour	121
Drove slowly or conspicuously (lights, sirens) to crimes in progress	*96*
Followed up on every pick-up complaint in 2nd half of tour	69
Ignored pick-up complaints from non-involved parties	*93*
Tried harder to get complainants to prosecute in 2nd half of tour	76
Tried to discourage complainants from pressing charges	*77*
Tried to take domestic incident jobs in 2nd half of tour	97
Avoided assignments to domestic incidents	*77*
Tried to handle jobs before telling dispatcher in 2nd half of tour	60
Tried to dispose of jobs without alerting dispatcher/supervisor	*71*

Note. Arrest-avoidance methods and their index scores are in italicized print. Maximum possible Index score is 400.

Interestingly, officers who make greater use of arrest-seeking methods for overtime do not necessarily make *less* use of arrest-avoiding methods for timely sign-out or processing aversion. Table 9-14, a correlation matrix of overall usage for the three types of adaptive behaviors, shows all associations to be significant and *positive*. Besides the expected high relationship between avoiding arrest for timely sign-out and avoiding it for processing aversion, there is a small correlation between arrest-seeking for overtime and arrest-avoidance for sign-out, and a smaller correlation between arrest-seeking for overtime and avoiding for processing aversion. This suggests that officers who are inclined to use arrest-control skills may apply them to both arrest-seeking and arrest-avoidance situations.

Table 9-14. *Correlation of Arrest-Seeking for Overtime, Arrest-Avoidance for Sign-Out, and Arrest-Avoidance for Processing Aversion* (N=506)

		Arrest-Avoidance for Timely Sign-Out	Arrest-Avoidance for Processing Aversion
Arrest-Seeking for Overtime	r_s	.15**	.10*
	n	493	492
Arrest-Avoidance for Timely Sign-Out	r_s		.67***
	n		498
*p < .05. **p < .01. ***p < .001.			

This section of the survey demonstrates how protracted processing can distort arrest behavior. Officers acknowledge using all the listed seeking and avoidance tactics, plus others that they themselves suggest. Some of the less-common strategies, such as focusing on minorities to arrest or driving slowly to a crime to allow the suspect to escape are clearly unethical.

In light of the officers' infrequent arrest-making, it is no surprise that arrest-seeking tactics overall are not widely used. Indeed, more than half of the respondents say they rarely or never use them. Arrest-seeking methods are more frequently employed by high-arrest officers and those working in the high-crime Bronx, and they are positively correlated with the need for arrest overtime money.

Arrest-avoidance techniques are far more common and are positively correlated with both the officers' need to get off work and their aversion to arrest processing. Compared to High-Arrest officers, No-Arresters use evasion strategies more extensively and are more motivated by their dislike of processing.

Attitudes toward Arrest

(Survey Item 56)

COMPSTAT: Great for City, bad for police officers because "shit rolls downhill." Pay: Awful, $940.00 a paycheck for 2 weeks—are you shitting me!!! Arrest Process: Printing Machines (livescan) are horrible & don't work half the time. OLBS computer can't log on because no code for it, so you spend 30 min. trying to find someone with a code. Central Booking: A bunch of miserable fucks, cops who treat you like shit, so you never want to put cuffs on anyone. Lieutenants to captains to chiefs have no balls to stand up for their cops...This department would be great if you just let cops do their jobs.

Participant 257

The above comment was just one of many in the survey expressing profound anger and bitterness toward arrest-making and the job in general. What role do such sentiments play in adaptive arrest behavior?

According to some descriptions of police culture, officers convey cynical attitudes toward work through oft-repeated "maxims" (Reuss-Ianni, 1983; Kappler et al., 1994). In my own experience, fellow officers seemed to rationalize self-interested arrest behavior by exchanging such maxims. These were either cynical comments about arrest or admonitions to put self and family first. Eight of such statements are presented in the survey's next section, interspersed with seven "professional" statements endorsing arrest-making as an important duty. Participants rate their level of agreement from 0 (*strongly disagree*) to 10 (*strongly agree*).

Table 10-1 arranges these 15 statements from highest to lowest mean agreement scores. Officers agree overall with seven out of eight cynical items and four out of seven professional items. The three most strongly endorsed statements (all scoring over 7) contend that officers' arrests are misused to further the reputations of, respectively, prosecutors, commanding officers, and politicians. At the other extreme, three of the four rejected statements (scoring below 5) claimed that arrests fulfilled valid civic objectives. And, although my coworkers had sometimes expressed nonchalance about the legality of specific arrests, survey participants agreed *least* with this attitude.

The mean agreement level for all cynical statements is 6.1 ($SD = 1.6$) and for all professional statements is 5.2 ($SD = 1.5$). The mean agreement levels for the two groups of statements display a correlation of -.13 ($N=497$,

$p = .003$) In other words, officers who hold stronger cynical or self-serving attitudes are slightly inclined to hold weaker professional attitudes.

Table 10-1. *Attitudes toward Arrests* (N = 506)

Item 56. Below are 15 statements. Each is followed by an opinion scale, wherein "0" indicates the strongest disagreement, "5" indicates a neutral position, and "10" indicates the strongest agreement. Please indicate the extent to which you agree or disagree with each statement along its scale.

Cynical (C) or Professional (P) Statement	C/P	N	Level of Agreement	SD
"ADAs will plea bargain a felony to a violation if it means an easy conviction."	C	489	7.8	4.3
"Arrest statistics are manipulated by the C.O. or higher brass to make themselves look good."	C	489	7.7	2.5
"Arrest policies depend more on 'politics' than on concepts of sound crime-fighting."	C	486	7.2	2.4
"No arrest is worth risking serious injury."	C	488	6.9	3.1
"A person who takes the oath of a police officer should be prepared to make sacrifices."	P	490	6.7	2.7
"Judges will accept almost any plea bargain just to clear their calendars."	C	488	6.2	2.6
"Arrests represent the way society enforces basic standards of right and wrong."	P	488	5.9	2.3
"Arrests for 'quality of life' offenses prevent more serious crime problems."	P	489	5.7	2.5
"It's no big deal if a perp gets away, as he'll get caught sooner or later doing something else."	C	489	5.5	3.0
"Making arrests isn't worth it if they really disrupt your home life."	C	488	5.4	3.0
"Making good arrests is a way for officers to advance in their career."	P	491	5.2	3.0
"Arrests show that the police are doing what the public expects of them."	P	490	4.9	2.5
"A good police officer should regularly make arrests."	P	490	4.6	2.8
"Arrests deter offenders from repeating their criminal behavior."	P	490	3.6	2.8
"Arresting on shaky legal grounds is o.k. if you figure that the perp got away with many other crimes."	C	486	2.2	2.7

Table 10-2. *Attitudes toward Arrest of No-Arrest and High-Arrest Officers*

Cynical (C) or Professional (P) Statement	C/P	No-Arrest Group (n=151)			High-Arrest Group (n=95)			T	df	p
		n	Level of Agreement	SD	n	Level of Agreement	SD			
"ADAs will plea bargain a felony to a violation if it means an easy conviction."	C	146	7.7	2.3	88	7.7	2.6	.25	232	.805
"Arrest statistics are manipulated by the C.O. or higher brass to make themselves look good."	C	147	7.8	2.7	88	7.7	2.5	.43	233	.670
"Arrest policies depend more on 'politics' than on concepts of sound crime-fighting."	C	145	7.3	2.6	87	6.9	2.5	1.18	230	.240
"No arrest is worth risking serious injury."	C	145	6.8	3.4	91	6.7	3.1	.29	234	.771
"A person who takes the oath of a police officer should be prepared to make sacrifices."	P	145	6.8	2.7	91	6.7	2.4	.45	211.0	.653
"Judges will accept almost any plea bargain just to clear their calendars."	C	147	6.1	2.8	88	6.5	2.5	-1.21	233	.227
"Arrests represent the way Society enforces basic standards of right and wrong."	P	146	6.0	2.5	88	5.9	2.3	.33	232	.738
"Arrests for 'quality of life' offenses prevent more serious crime problems."	**P**	**146**	**5.4**	**2.7**	**88**	**6.4**	**2.5**	**-2.78**	**232**	**.006**
"It's no big deal if a perp gets away, as he'll get caught sooner or later doing something else."	C	144	5.6	3.2	91	5.4	2.9	.61	206.8	.546
"Making arrests isn't worth it if they really disrupt your home life."	C	147	5.6	3.2	88	5.3	2.7	.702	203.9	.484
"Making good arrests is a way for officers to advance in their career."	P	148	5.0	3.1	88	5.4	2.9	-1.06	234	.292
"Arrests show that the police are doing what the public expects of them."	P	144	4.7	2.6	91	4.8	2.6	-.302	233	.763
"A good police officer should regularly make arrests."	**P**	**147**	**3.8**	**2.5**	**88**	**5.7**	**2.5**	**-5.36**	**233**	**<.001**
"Arrests deter offenders from repeating their criminal behavior."	P	147	3.4	2.9	88	3.7	2.9	-.65	233	.516
"Arresting on shaky legal grounds is ok if you figure that the perp got away with many other crimes."	C	146	2.1	2.7	88	1.8	2.4	.81	232	.421

Note. Boldface rows denote statements for which the agreement levels of No-Arrest and High-Arrest groups are significantly different.

Table 10-2 compares the attitudes of officers in the No-Arrest and High-Arrest groups. For 13 out of 15 statements, agreement levels are essentially the same. Only the professional principles that good officers make arrests and that minor arrests can prevent more serious crimes garner significantly more support from High-Arrest officers. The mean scores for all cynical statements are 6.1 (SD = 1.8, n = 148) for the No-Arresters and 6.0 (SD = 1.4, n = 92) for the High-Arresters, a statistical match: t (222.8) = .74, p >.05. However, the average for all professional statements is 5.0 (SD = 1.5, n = 148) for the No-Arrest group, significantly lower than the 5.4 (SD = 1.5, n = 93) for the High-Arrest group: t (239) = -2.03, p = .044.

Overall, then, the No-Arrest and High-Arrest officers are in common agreement on all of the cynical statements but not all of the professional ones. The High-Arrest group alone feel that regular arrest making is essential to good police work, and it had greater faith that arrest-making could deter crime. Thus, overtime motives aside, the High-Arrest officers seem driven to arrest by a higher sense of purpose.

But are officers with more cynical or self-serving attitudes toward arrests also more inclined to use adaptive arrest behaviors? Are officers with more positive, professional attitudes *less* likely to use them? As discussed in Chapter 9, adaptive arrest behaviors can take the form of arrest-seeking measures aimed at overtime, and arrest-avoidance measures aimed at timely sign-out or escaping processing difficulties. If adaptive arrest behaviors are encouraged by the acceptance of cynical maxims, and *dis*couraged by the acceptance of professional ones, then we should find more such behaviors in the first instance and less in the second.

Table 10-3 displays the Spearman correlations of officers' mean level of agreement with cynical statements with the three forms of adaptive behavior. All are significant and positive, as predicted. The r_s values indicate that negative arrest attitudes have greater association with arrest-avoidance than with arrest-seeking behaviors, probably because the eight cynical arrest statements argue far more forcefully *against* making arrests.

Table 10-3. *Correlations of Cynical Arrest Attitudes and Adaptive Arrest Behaviors* (N = 506)

Adaptive Behavior	N	r_s	P
Arrest-Seeking for Overtime	491	.13	.004
Arrest-Avoidance for Timely Sign-out	495	.36	<.001
Arrest-Avoidance for Processing Burdens	494	.37	<.001

The second question, whether adaptive arrest behavior is negatively associated with professional arrest attitudes, is addressed in Table 10-4. It indicates that arrest overtime-seeking is *not* significantly related to professional attitudes. However, conforming to expectation, both types of arrest *avoidance* display significant negative correlations with professional attitudes. In other words, the less the officers subscribed to the professional maxims, the more they use avoidance measures.

Table 10-4. *Correlations of Professional Arrest Attitudes and Adaptive Arrest Behaviors* (N = 506)

Adaptive Behavior	N	r_s	P
Arrest-Seeking for Overtime	491	.01	.782
Arrest-Avoidance for Timely Sign-out	495	-.22	<.001
Arrest-Avoidance for Processing Burdens	494	-.24	<.001

The results in Table 10-4 may reflect the influence of High-Arrest officers, who tend to subscribe more to professional attitudes (Table 10-2) but also tend to use more overtime-seeking methods (Table 9-3). By raising the overall professionalism score of the entire Core Sample, the High-Arrest officers erase the predicted negative correlation between professional beliefs and overtime-seeking.

From this section on arrest-related attitudes, we learn that officers hold both cynical and professional beliefs but more strongly endorse cynical ones. Those with stronger cynical attitudes are slightly more likely to hold weaker professional attitudes.

Three cynical statements, contending that arrests are manipulated to further the careers of prosecutors, commanding officers, and politicians, drew the highest levels of agreement. Conversely, three of the four professional statements—that arrests are the mark of a good police officer, fulfill public expectations, and deter offenders from repeating their crime— were rejected as false.

No-Arrest and High-Arrest officers are essentially in agreement for all eight cynical arrest statements, and five of seven professional arrest statements. Where the High-Arrest group differ is in its endorsement of the professional principles that good officers make arrests and that minor arrests can prevent more serious crimes.

Officers with stronger cynical attitudes toward arrest use more adaptive behaviors, particularly to avoid arrest. Officers with weaker professional attitudes toward arrest also reported more adaptive behavior but *only* to avoid arrest, not to seek it.

Most research on police attitudes finds that they are only weakly connected to officer behavior (National Academy of Sciences, 2004). In that context, the findings that more professional attitudes toward arrest are found in high-arrest officers, and that more cynical attitudes toward arrest correlate with the use of arrest-avoidance tactics, stand out.

CHAPTER ELEVEN

Personal Needs Among Other Arrest Determinants
(Survey Item 40)

Depending on the reason(s) you decide to get on this dog dictates your approach to making arrests. Some people are more for the money. Others are here for benefits, and few are here for sense of duty, etc.

Participant 151

We saw in Chapter 2 that researchers link arrest decisions to dozens of variables. The next survey section seeks to place officers' personal concerns within the context of these other arrest-related factors. It presents a list of concerns that intersperses 15 personal considerations with 17 situational and organizational arrest variables drawn from previous studies. Participants rate how often, in a possible arrest situation, each factor is important in their decision to arrest or not arrest. By comparing *Importance Index* scores for the 31 items (calculated in the same manner as the previous indexes), the relative decision-making "weight" of each variable can be gauged.

Table 11-1 reveals that all 31 variables have influence, an indication of the true complexity of the arrest decision. The situational variables of offense seriousness, suspect demeanor, and complainant cooperation and attitude are the most salient determinants, echoing many previous studies. But ranked just below these factors are the officers' needs to get off work for a social commitment (#5), and their reluctance to deal with a difficult, dangerous, filthy, or sick prisoner (#6). The next factor, number of sectors running (#7), stems from concern that an arrest will take the officer off patrol for the entire tour, sometimes overburdening coworkers. Also high on the list (#8) is the need to make overtime money.

In the middle third of the rankings are seven more personal variables. A request to accommodate the arrest-making needs of a coworker (#12) led this group. Next is the likelihood of complex or protracted arrest processing, and of equal importance is the prospect of a tour change to accommodate the ADA or judge (often reverting to straight-time pay). This factor is directly followed by the need to get off work on time for a child-related activity. Also in this middle grouping is the lack of a coworker to take the officer's arrest so that the participant's intervention would inevitably mean "getting stuck." This is matched in importance by the desire

Table 11-1. *Arrest Factors Listed in Order of Importance Index Scores* (N = 506)

Item 40. Below are factors officers may weigh while on routine patrol when faced with a possible arrest situation. Please indicate how often these factors are important in your own decision to arrest or not arrest while on routine patrol.

Factor	N	Never	Rarely	Sometimes	Often	Always	Importance Index[a]
1. Level/seriousness of the offense	492	10%	10%	22%	22%	35%	260
2. Willingness of complainant to prosecute	489	11%	15%	41%	25%	16%	210
3. Attitude/demeanor of the suspect	492	14%	16%	43%	19%	8%	191
4. Attitude/demeanor of complainant/victim	490	15%	22%	44%	14%	5%	172
5. Need to get off work on time for social commitment	493	18%	21%	40%	14%	7%	171
6. Difficult / dangerous / filthy / sick prisoner	491	20%	21%	40%	11%	8%	167
7. Manpower / number of sectors running	490	22%	22%	35%	14%	7%	162
8. Need to make overtime money	489	23%	25%	33%	10%	10%	161
9. Pressure from supervisor / CO to make arrest	489	27%	24%	28%	13%	8%	151
10. Presence of supervisor	491	26%	32%	30%	7%	6%	137
11. Presence of bystanders / personal safety	487	24%	31%	33%	7%	4%	134
12. Request to take coworker's arrest/give away your arrest	492	26%	29%	40%	3%	3%	130
13. Long/complicated paperwork or processing	492	33%	29%	25%	6%	7%	125
14. Likeliness of being rescheduled to see ADA/go to court	492	35%	28%	24%	7%	7%	125
15. Need to get off work on time for child-related activity	492	45%	14%	23%	8 %	9%	120
16. Desires/expectations of community	490	38%	30%	24%	7%	2%	113
17. Lack of another officer to take your arrest	492	33%	35%	28%	3%	2%	108
18. Desire to go into station house / take break from patrol	490	38%	27%	29%	5%	2%	108
19. Need to make comp time	487	39%	30%	23%	5%	4%	107
20. Class / type of suspect (derelict, blue-collar, VIP, etc.)	493	40%	27%	25%	7%	2%	105
21. Pressure to limit overtime	487	44%	26%	18%	6%	6%	104
22. Class of complainant (homeless, blue-collar, VIP, etc.)	493	40%	25%	28%	4%	2%	101
23. Judgment /opinions of other officers	488	38%	32%	24%	4%	2%	100
24. Desire for career advancement / plain-clothes assignment	489	47%	23%	219%	5%	6%	100

Factor	N	Never	Rarely	Some-times	Often	Always	Importance Index[a]
25. Need to carpool / beat rush hour / catch train, / etc.	491	51%	17%	19%	8%	5%	99
26. Bad weather	490	43%	27%	25%	3%	1%	90
27. Boredom	490	46%	30%	20%	2%	1%	80
28. Pedigree of suspect (race, sex, age, etc.)	492	52%	29%	14%	3%	2%	74
29. Need to get off work on time for second job	491	65%	12%	14%	6%	4%	74
30. Pedigree of complainant (race, sex, age, etc.)	488	53%	27%	16%	3%	1%	72
31. Need to get off work on time for college-related activity	488	75%	11%	10%	3%	2%	48

Note. Boldface items indicate personal or self-interested factors.
[a]Row sum of (percent of officers each frequency category) x (frequency of importance level). Frequency of importance scored from 0 (Never) to 4 (Always). Maximum possible Index score is 400. Order of equal scores is arbitrarily assigned.

to go into the station house or take a break from patrol. Just a point lower is the need to earn comp time.

In the bottom third of the list are the remaining five personal variables, respectively: commuting concerns, bad weather, boredom, and sign-out need for a second job or college. That the commuting factor is ranked relatively low (#26) suggests that it has a more limited impact on arrest decisions than was implied by its frequency as a post-work concern (Table 7-2). In contrast, the rankings for need to go to a second job or college are more in line with the low concern Index scores found previously.

Also noteworthy is that some of the most-studied situational variables are surpassed in importance by personal ones. Of the 31 arrest factors, suspect class or type is ranked #20, complainant class or type is #22, suspect race, sex, or age is #28 (after boredom and bad weather), and complainant race, sex, or age is #30.

Separate Index scores for No-Arrest and High-Arrest officers are also calculated and ranked, to see if the two groups accord different weights to the 31 arrest factors. Table 11-2 indicates that is indeed the case. For instance, the most important personal variable for No-Arrest officers is "Difficult/dangerous/filthy/sick prisoner" (5th place, as compared to the High-Arrest group's 9th place). The No-Arrest group also assigns far higher importance than the High-Arrest group to the arrest-suppressing considerations of "paperwork/processing" (9th place versus 26th place) and "child-related activity" (12th place versus 20th place), and to the arrest-augmenting factor, "pressure from supervisors/CO" (2nd place versus 10th place).

In contrast, the most important personable variable for High-Arrest officers is the "need to make overtime money." It held 2nd place among all variables, while for No-Arresters it was down in 14th place. High-Arresters rated the desire for career advancement or plainclothes assignment as an important arrest-making factor (8th place), while the No-Arresters barely considered it (30th place).

Table 11-2. *Importance Index Scores and Rankings of Arrest Factors for No-Arrest and High-Arrest Officers*

Factor	No-Arrest Group (n = 151)		High-Arrest Group (n = 94)	
	Importance Index Score[a]	Importance Rank	Importance Index Score[a]	Importance Rank
1 Level/seriousness of the offense	263	1st	271	1st
2 Willingness of complainant to prosecute	203	3rd	207	3rd
3. Attitude/demeanor of the suspect	187	4th	195	4th
4. Attitude/demeanor of complainant/victim	155	8th	182	5th
5. **Need to get off work on time for social commitment**	180	6th	162	6th
6. **Difficult / dangerous / filthy / sick prisoner**	185	5th	143	9th
7. Manpower / number of sectors running	160	7th	162	7th
8. **Need to make overtime money**	132	14th	212	2nd
9. Pressure from supervisor / CO to make arrest	214	2nd	139	10th
10. Presence of supervisor	148	11th	119	14th
11. Presence of bystanders / personal safety	149	10th	130	11th
12. **Request to take coworker's arrest/give away** your arrest	137	13th	126	12th
14. **Long/complicated paperwork or processing**	152	9th	80	26th
13. **Likeliness of being rescheduled to see** ADA/go to court	127	15th	113	15th
15. **Need to get off work on time for child-** related activity	143	12th	101	20th
16. Desires/expectations of community	112	18th	92	23rd

Factor	No-Arrest Group (n = 151)		High-Arrest Group (n = 94)	
	Importance Index Score[a]	Importance Rank	Importance Index Score[a]	Importance Rank
17. Lack of another officer to take your arrest	113	17th	97	21st
18. Desire to go into station house / take break from patrol	98	21st	109	16th
19. Need to make comp time	94	24th	121	13th
20. Class / type of suspect (derelict, blue-collar, VIP, etc)	115	16th	76	27th
21. Pressure to limit overtime	108	19th	109	17th
22. Class of complainant (homeless, blue-collar, VIP, etc.)	108	20th	90	25th
23. Judgment /opinions of other officers	97	22nd	97	22nd
24. Desire for career advancement / plainclothes assignment	67	30th	147	8th
25. Need to carpool / beat rush hour / catch train / etc.	97	23rd	91	24ph
26. Bad weather	81	27th	108	18th
27. Boredom	80	28th	101	19th
28. Pedigree of suspect (race, sex, age, etc.)	86	25th	58	29th
29. Need to get off work on time for second job	71	29th	57	30th
30. Pedigree of complainant (race, sex, age, etc.)	84	26th	62	28th
31. Need to get off work on time for college-related activity	42	31st	53	31st

In summarizing this section's findings, it should again be noted that the Index scores are not amenable to statistical tests for significance. However, one indication of their validity is that the top-ranked concerns of crime seriousness, complainant cooperation, and suspect demeanor are consistent with other research. That personal arrest variables like social commitments, prisoner problems, and overtime also rank highly is strong evidence that they carry considerable weight. Moreover, even mid-ranked personal concerns such as difficult paperwork, being rescheduled, and attending to children are rated more important than such well-studied arrest determinants as community expectations and suspects' physical or class traits. Also telling are the differences between No-Arrest and High-

Arrest officers. The No-Arresters are more influenced by prisoner difficulties, complicated procedures, needy children, and supervisory pressure, the High-Arresters by overtime money and career advancement.

CHAPTER TWELVE

The Impotence of Management

(Survey Items 61–73)

Based on research and personal observations, I believe several factors make it hard for police management to curb self-serving arrest behavior. These are (1) the absence of supervisors at the scene of potential arrests, (2) the reluctance of supervisors to reverse subordinates' arrest decisions, (3) the ineffectiveness of sanctions to limit high overtime, and (4) the ineffectiveness of sanctions to encourage arrest-making. This section of the survey examines whether these managerial weaknesses allow adaptive arrest behavior to continue.

SUPERVISORY PRESENCE

Asked to select, to the nearest 10%, how often their supervisor is present *before* they place an individual under arrest, participants respond with a mean score of 32.7% (SD = 26.4, N = 433). Asked how often their supervisor was present when they *decline* a legitimate arrest, officers offer a mean response of 24.8% (SD = 22.8, N = 323). That is, a supervisor is present for less than a third of the arrests made and less than a quarter of the declined arrests. This leaves ample opportunity for officers to weigh personal priorities in their arrest decisions.

That supervisors are more likely to be present when an arrest is made than when it is declined is not surprising. As we have seen, officers will make an arrest if prodded by a supervisor, but they generally are inclined to avoid arrest-making in discretionary situations. Their popular expression, *shitcanning an arrest*, implies a swift and discrete disposal, known only to other officers at the scene.

SUPERVISORY CHALLENGES TO OFFICER DECISIONS

Officers also are asked to estimate to the nearest 10% how often their supervisor overrules their choice to make or to decline an arrest. The mean frequency for reversals of officer decisions *to arrest* is only 6.8% (SD = 13.1, N = 459), with 64.9% of officers reporting that such decisions are *never* overruled. The mean for reversals of officer decisions *to decline arrest* is 21.0% of the time (SD = 23.7, N = 459), with 30.3% reporting that this had never occurred. Thus, it is apparent that supervisors rarely countermand the arrest decisions of their subordinates. And, as we would expect from officers' arrest-avoidance tendencies, supervisors are more likely to order an arrest than to quash one.

SANCTIONS AGAINST OVERTIME

Commanding officers are held strictly accountable for overtime spending and pressure both supervisors and officers to keep overtime within specified limits. Yet, in my observations, officers who were sanctioned for earning high overtime reacted in ways that defeated management's intent.

To gauge how participants respond to overtime control policies, they are first asked how often they exceed management's monthly overtime caps. Figure 12-1 shows that 53.2% (256 officers) have never run afoul of these limits. A small, distinct group composing 6.9% (33 officers) are over quota every month. The mean for all officers is just 2.6 times in 12 months ($SD = 3.6$), in keeping with participants' low overall arrest rates. For the 225 officers who went over the limit at least once, the mean is 5.5 times ($SD = 3.4$).

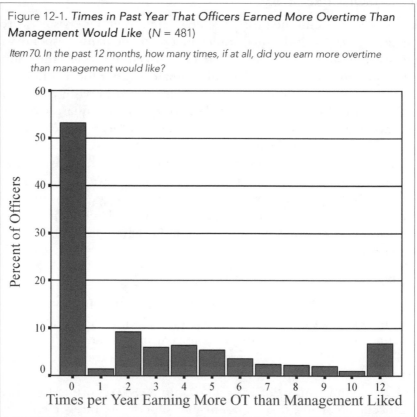

Figure 12-1. *Times in Past Year That Officers Earned More Overtime Than Management Would Like* (N = 481)

Item 70. In the past 12 months, how many times, if at all, did you earn more overtime than management would like?

Those who report earning arrest overtime *after* being "capped out" are then asked to chose which if any sanction(s) they experienced from a list of possible consequences. Table 12-1 presents these results, ordered from the most to the least common sanction. The table shows that despite labor regulations and contractual agreements, the most frequent managerial sanction for high overtime is to pressure officers to select payment in time. The next most frequent managerial responses are to do nothing at all to the officers. Most of the other sanctions, however, can feel quite punitive to the officer involved.

Table 12-1. *Sanctions Imposed on Officers for Excess Overtime* (n = 225)

Item 71. The following is a list of consequences that police management may threaten, or actually impose, for making too much cash overtime. Please indicate any consequence(s) you experienced.

Sanction	N	Valid %
Was pressured to take overtime in compensation time rather than cash	77	61.6%
No consequences for making a lot of overtime	66	29.3%
Was admonished by Integrity Control Officer (ICO) or other superior	64	28.4%
Was threatened with reassignment/tour change/RDO change	50	22.2%
Was denied details or special assignments that offered overtime	47	20.9%
Was denied time off	44	19.6%
Had arrests reassigned to another officer	40	17.8%
Was reassigned or given tour change/RDO change	38	16.9%
Was given lower evaluation	37	16.4%
Was threatened to not be able to work with steady partner	35	15.6%
Was given fewer patrol assignments with arrest opportunities	34	15.1%
Was forbidden to work with steady partner	34	15.1%
Other: "*Given other duties while processing arrest*"; "*Not paid enough*"	2	0.9%

Note. Participants were told to select as many choices as apply.

Do these sanctions evoke the desired response of less arrest-making on overtime? Participants are asked, after each consequence they selected, to identify their own reaction(s) to that sanction. Their possible responses are: (1) Did everything the same; (2) Made fewer arrests close to the end of tour; (3) Made fewer arrests generally; (4) Took overtime in comp time; (5) Tried to make *more* arrest overtime to make up for lost income; (6) Got PBA delegate involved/filed grievance; (7) Tried to get transfer to other unit; (8) Took second job/worked more at second job; and (9) Other.

Table 12-2. Officer Reactions to Sanctions Imposed for Exceeding Overtime Limit (n = 225)

Sanction Imposed	Officer Reactions to Imposed Sanctions (Frequency and % of Total for Sanction)								Multiple Responses (1 each unless indicated)	Total Responses
	a) Did Everything the Same	b) Made Fewer Arrests Generally	c) Got Union Involved/ Filed Grievance	d) Took OT in Comp Time	e) Tried to Make More Arrests	f) Tried to Get Transfer to Other Unit	g) Made Fewer Arrests at EOT	h) Took 2nd job/Worked More at 2nd job		
Was pressured to take overtime in time rather than cash	30 (33.0%)	11 (12.1%)	10 (11.0%)	22 (24.2%)	7 (7.7%)	4 (4.4%)	5 (5.5%)	2 (2.2%)	b-c, b-d (2), b-g, c-d (2), d-e, d-f, d-h, f-g, c-f-h, c-d-e-h	91
No consequences for making a lot of overtime	47 (70.1%)	6 (9.0%)	3 (4.5%)	4 (6.0%)	4 (6.0%)	0 (0.0%)	3 (4.5%)	0 (0.0%)	b-g, b-h	67
Was admonished by ICO or other superior	31 (44.9%)	11 (15.9%)	6 (8.7%)	7 (10.1%)	5 (7.2%)	1 (1.4%)	3 (4.3%)	5 (7.2%)	b-c, b-h, d-h, b-d-g, c-d-e-h	69
Was threatened w. reassignment/ tour change / RDO change	27 (50.9%)	5 (9.4%)	8 (15.1%)	3 (5.7%)	3 (5.7%)	3 (5.7%)	0 (0.0%)	4 (7.5%)	b-c, b-c-f, c-d-f	53
Was denied details or special assignments that offered OT	21 (46.7%)	6 (13.3%)	4 (8.9%)	4 (8.9%)	4 (8.9%)	2 (4.4%)	0 (0.0%)	4 (8.9%)	b-h, c-d, d-h, e-h	45
Was denied time off	21 (48.8%)	9 (20.9%)	10 (23.0%)	1 (2.3%)	1 (2.3%)	1 (2.3%)	0 (0.0%)	0 (0.0%)	b-c, c-d	43
Had arrests reassigned to another officer	27 (62.8%)	5 (11.6%)	2 (4.7%)	1 (2.3%)	1 (2.3%)	2 (4.7%)	5 (11.6%)	0 (0.0%)	b-c, f-g	43
Was reassigned or given tour change / RDO change	21 (52.5%)	4 (10.0%)	6 (15.0%)	0 (0.0%)	4 (10.0%)	2 (5.0%)	2 (5.0%)	1 (2.5%)	c-e, c-h, b-c-f	40
Was given lower evaluation	20 (43.5%)	10 (22.2%)	8 (17.4%)	0 (0.0%)	2 (4.7%)	4 (8.7%)	1 (2.2%)	1 (2.2%)	b-c, b-g, c-f, b-c-f, b-e-f, c-f-h	46
Was threatened to not be able to work with steady partner	24 (60.0%)	9 (22.5%)	3 (7.5%)	1 (2.5%)	1 (2.5%)	2 (5.0%)	0 (0.0%)	0 (0.0%)	b-c, b-d, c-f-h	40
Was given fewer patrol assignments with arrest opportunities	25 (67.6%)	3 (8.1%)	4 (10.8%)	0 (0.0%)	2 (5.4%)	3 (8.1%)	0 (0.0%)	0 (0.0%)	b-c, e-f, c-f-h	37
Was forbidden to work with steady partner	20 (52.6%)	7 (18.4%)	6 (15.8%)	0 (0.0%)	3 (7.9%)	1 (2.6%)	0 (0.0%)	1 (2.6%)	b-c, b-c-f	38
Frequency of Reaction	313 (51.2%)	86 (14.1%)	70 (11.5%)	43 (7.0%)	37 (6.1%)	25 (4.1%)	19 (3.1%)	18 (2.9%)	--	611

Note: Participants were told to select as many responses as apply. Where multiple responses were reported, each response also was included in the row total for that response.

Officer reactions to each sanction appear in Table 12-2, ordered from left to right by the overall frequencies of each reaction (bottom row). The table shows that after every imposed sanction, the most frequent officer response is to *do everything the same as before*. Over half of the responses overall are this non-reaction. Another quarter of officer responses are either to make fewer arrests generally and/or to complain to the union. And, about 13% defiantly aim for more arrests, tried to leave their unit, or put in more time at a second job. Clearly, these are not the effects the anti-overtime sanctions are intended to achieve.

Management can claim some limited success. When it directly pressures officers to opt for comp time instead of cash (the most common sanction), 24.2% of officers comply. In the face of all anti-overtime sanctions, 7.0% of officer reactions involve accepting time over money, and another 3.1% entail decreasing arrest-making at the end of tour. About a tenth of officer reactions achieve the goal of curtailing overtime costs. But overall, the sanctions imposed to curb arrest overtime are mostly counter-productive.

SANCTIONS TO ENCOURAGE ARREST-MAKING

Commanding officers are expected to ensure that each patrol officer performs at least some enforcement activity. Usually they are satisfied by an adequate number of summonses, but occasionally they will pressure officers for an arrest. Many officers understand this as a "quota" of one arrest per quarter-year, although some are expected to make more arrests to address a specific precinct condition.

To evaluate how management's arrest-boosting efforts affect participants, they first are asked how often supervisors tell them to make more arrests. Figure 12-2 indicates that 39.6% (178 officers) had been addressed by a supervisor for low arrest activity at least once in the past year. The mean number of times for the entire group is 1.9 (SD = 3.1), but for the 178 participants who were criticized, the mean number of warnings was 4.8 (SD = 3.4).

Those who were urged to make more arrests are then asked which consequences they experienced, if any, from a list of choices. Table 12-3 orders these sanctions from the most to the least frequently chosen.

To find out if these sanctions have the desired effect of increasing arrests, participants are again asked to select their reaction(s) to each consequence. The list of possible responses are: (1) Did everything the same; (2) Made one routine arrest that month; (3) Made arrest for an offense that might otherwise get a summons; (4) Tried to "milk" the next arrest to

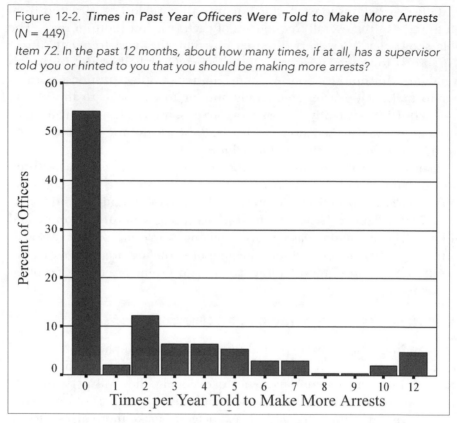

Figure 12-2. *Times in Past Year Officers Were Told to Make More Arrests* (N = 449)

Item 72. In the past 12 months, about how many times, if at all, has a supervisor told you or hinted to you that you should be making more arrests?

make it worth the effort; (5) Made enough arrests to show "average" activity; (6) Tried to get steady "inside" assignment; (7) Got PBA delegate involved/filed grievance; and (8) Other.

Table 12-4, like Table 12-2, shows that for every sanction, officers most often respond by making no change in their behavior. Overall, 54.1% "did everything the same." The next most common reaction is making a single, routine arrest, pursuant to a direct order or to a threat of reassignment, tour change, or change in regular days off (RDO). Overall, responses that entailed the increased arrest-making sought by management—either making one routine arrest or making an average number of arrests—represent only 24.3% of reactions.

Table 12-3. *Sanctions Imposed on Officers Making Insufficient Arrests* (n = 178)

Item 73. The following is a list of consequences that police management may threaten or actually imposed, for not making enough arrests. Please indicate any consequence(s) you experienced.

Sanction	N	Valid %
Was threatened with reassignment / tour change / RDO change	64	36.0%
Was told to take a specific arrest (e.g., shoplifter, reassigned arrest)	62	34.8%
Was denied time off	54	30.3%
Was given undesirable posts	53	29.8%
No consequences threatened or imposed	52	29.2%
Was given lower evaluation	49	27.5%
Was threatened to not be able to work with steady partner	47	26.4%
Was threatened with transfer	40	22.5%
Was reassigned / had tour changed / had RDO changed	38	21.3%
Was denied details or special assignments offering overtime	31	14.4%
Was threatened with loss of permission to work second job	27	15.2%
Was forbidden to work with steady partner	27	12.2%
Lost permission to work second job	26	14.6%
Was transferred	25	14.0%
Other (1 each): *Assigned to hospitalized prisoner every day for two months* *Walked solo foot post on midnights for four months* *Threatened with possible foot post* *Threatened with assigned arrest* *Was asked to try and make arrests* *Was told no overtime if don't make arrest in quarter* *Had a late job one day & scumbag sergeant refused to sign overtime slip*	7	3.9%

Note. Participants were told to select as many choices as apply.

Though 33 officers (5.3%) report "other reactions," only five specify what these are. In two comments, the officers seem chastened: "Wanted to go back to patrol and not be threatened to lose your chart days and RDOs"; "Took it into consideration and started to look further." Three are unrepentant: "Did less of everything"; "Gave no activity for several months"; and "Don't care what they do—still will get paid no matter what assignment you get." From a management perspective, over three-quarters of officer reactions are undesirable.

The array of measures used by police supervisors to control adaptive arrest behaviors—being present at arrest situations, countermanding in-appropriate arrest decisions, reassigning late-in-tour arrests, and sanctioning high overtime or low arrest-making—all appear to have little effect. What then can be done to change arrest behavior to better serve justice and public safety?

Table 12-4. Officer Reactions to Sanctions Imposed for Insufficient Arrests (N = 178)

Sanction Imposed	Officer Reactions to Imposed Sanctions (Frequency and Percent of Total for Sanction)									
	a. Did Everything the Same	b. Made One Routine Arrest that Month	c. Made Enough Arrests to show Avg. Activity	d. Got Union Involved/ Filed Grievance	e. Tried to Milk Next Arrest to Make it Worth the Effort	f. Other Reactions	g. Made Arrest for Offense Eligible for Summons	h. Tried to Get Steady inside Assignment	Multiple Responses (1 each unless indicated)	Total Responses
Is threatened with reassignment / tour change / RDO change	30 (43.5%)	15 (21.7%)	8 (11.6%)	3 (4.3%)	2 (2.9%)	6 (8.7%)	2 (2.9%)	3 (4.3%)	b-e (2), g-c, g-h, h-f	69
Is told to take a specific arrest (e.g., shoplifter, reassigned arrest)	27 (42.2%)	12 (18.8%)	8 (12.5%)	0 (0%)	11 (17.2%)	4 (6.3%)	2 (3.1%)	0 (0%)	b-e, b-c	64
Is denied time off	26 (44.8%)	5 (8.6%)	9 (15.5%)	8 (13.8%)	1 (1.7%)	4 (6.9%)	3 (5.2%)	2 (3.4%)	b-g, c-d, g-h, e-c	58
No consequences threatened/imposed	38 (66.7%)	7 (12.3%)	8 (14.0%)	2 (3.5%)	0 (0%)	1 (1.8%)	1 (1.8%)	0 (0%)	b-g, b-c (2), b-c-d	57
Is given undesirable posts.	29 (51.8%)	9 (16.1%)	4 (7.1%)	2 (3.6%)	6 (10.7%)	3 (5.4%)	2 (3.6%)	1 (1.8%)	b-g-e, b-e, c-g	56
Is given lower evaluation	26 (48.1%)	8 (14.8%)	9 (16.7%)	2 (3.7%)	3 (5.6%)	2 (3.7%)	3 (5.6%)	1 (1.9%)	b-e (2), b-g, g-e, g-c	54
Is threatened to not be able to work with steady partner	30 (62.5%)	7 (14.6%)	4 (8.3%)	3 (6.3%)	1 (2.1%)	2 (4.2%)	1 (2.1%)	0 (0%)	b-e	48
Is threatened with transfer	23 (57.5%)	4 (10.0%)	2 (5.0%)	6 (15.0%)	1 (2.5%)	1 (2.5%)	2 (5.0%)	1 (2.5%)	g-c, g-h, e-d	40
Is reassigned / had tour changed / had RDO changed	19 (47.5%)	9 (22.5%)	2 (5.0%)	3 (7.5%)	2 (5.0%)	3 (7.5%)	1 (2.5%)	1 (2.5%)	b-g-e	40
Is denied details or special assignments offering overtime	20 (64.5%)	3 (9.7%)	3 (9.7%)	2 (6.5%)	0 (0%)	3 (9.7%)	0 (0%)	0 (0%)	--	31
Is threatened with loss of permission to work second job	19 (65.5%)	4 (13.8%)	2 (6.9%)	0 (0%)	3 (10.3%)	1 (3.4%)	0 (0%)	0 (0%)	b-e, e-c	29
Is forbidden to work with steady partner	17 (60.7%)	4 (14.3%)	1 (3.6%)	4 (14.3%)	1 (3.6%)	1 (3.6%)	0 (0%)	0 (0%)	b-e	28
Lost permission to work 2nd job	18 (72.0%)	1 (4.0%)	2 (8.0%)	1 (4.0%)	1 (4.0%)	1 (4.0%)	0 (0%)	0 (0%)	--	25
Is transferred	16 (61.5%)	1 (3.8%)	1 (3.8%)	5 (19.2%)	1 (3.8%)	1 (3.8%)	0 (0%)	1 (3.8%)	b-e	26
Frequency of Reaction	338 (54.1%)	89 (14.2%)	63 (10.1%)	42 (6.7%)	33 (5.3%)	33 (5.3%)	17 (2.7%)	10 (1.6%)	--	625

Note. Participants were told to select as many responses as apply Where multiple responses were reported, each response also is included in the row total for that response.

CHAPTER THIRTEEN

Fixing the Problem

I think arrest processing should be done like other big cities—you write a 61 and drop them off and resume patrol. You should have civilians do paperwork and Corrections do the transports from beginning to end! The P.D. can take their overtime because when my tour ends I want to be away from the precinct!

Participant # 251

Several survey comments express awareness that there are quicker and easier ways to process arrests in other police departments. How many agencies have streamlined arrest procedures that minimally influence arrest behavior? How many experience delays and difficulties like those of NYPD? What can other agencies teach America's largest police department?

To address these issues, a brief survey of arrest processing practices (Appendix C) was addressed to 253 police departments in U.S. cities with more than 100,000 residents. Mailed in June 2002, it elicited 130 responses, a 51.4% return rate.

The survey's introduction, offering a brief description of the NYPD's processing problems, elicited expressions of amazement. One supervisor wrote, "If an arrest took over seven hours in this department, my officers would crucify me—and rightly so!" Another had this reaction:

> Your chief has dropped the ball. Scrap your way of doing things & start over. Processing time should *never* be a factor in an arrest decision—what about the victims? This practice is unethical and is symptomatic of a sick system.

The participating agencies, asked the duration of their own arrest procedures, provide different types of responses, as displayed in Table 13-1. Many respondents who report a range of times explain that their lengthier procedures reflect arrests for drunk driving or more serious, complicated crimes. The mean lengths clearly indicate that processing can be done in a lot less time than it takes in New York:

Table 13-1. *Length of Arrest Processing in Other Large U.S. Cities* (N = 130)				
Type of Response	# of PDs	Range	Mean	SD
Typical Length	57	30 min. –5 hrs.	1.74 hrs.	1.09
Minimum Length	74	5 min. –5 hrs.	1.15 hrs.	0.83
Maximum Length	71	45 min.–12 hrs[a]	3.39 hrs.	2.26
Not Known / It Depends	5	-	-	-
[a] Hilo, Hawaii's estimated maximum of 12 hours is offset by its minimum of 30 minutes				

Because about half of the surveys were not returned, it is impossible to know how many larger cities have difficulties similar to those of the NYPD. However, it must be noted that the Los Angeles Police Department also seems to have a processing problem. Its spokesperson wrote that it is "unrealistic" for the LAPD to be expected to compile valid statistics on processing time and that "since our Regional jail facilities accommodate other law enforcement agencies, a longer wait time is often generated." (Coincidentally, NYPD Central Booking personnel also make the claim that "it's those other agencies coming here that slow us down.")

A number of agencies say that their typical arrests involve little or no overtime. All report that arrest overtime is always paid at time-and-a-half rates in money or compensatory time.

The survey also finds that 112 of the departments, or 86.2%, used other personnel to assist the arresting officer in processing. Their roles are shown in Table 13-2. Particularly striking is the finding that in 71.5% of these agencies, *all* booking procedures are performed by personnel other than the arresting officer.

Table 13-2. *Arrest Processing Assistance in Other Large U.S. Cities* (*N* = 130)

Type of Assistance	# of PDs	Percent
Fingerprinting	67	51.5%
Retrieving Criminal Records (Rap Sheets)	23	17.7%
Taking Photos	41	31.5%
Guarding Prisoner	8	6.2%
Transporting Prisoners	42	32.3%
Handling Prisoners in/awaiting Court	33	25.4%
Data Entry	41	31.5%
Every Procedure	93	71.5%

In light of the computer and equipment problems in NYPD arrest processing, the survey asks other agencies about their use of technology. Table 13-3 displays a variety of applications.

What lessons do other police agencies offer the NYPD? First, processing duties can be readily performed by personnel other than the arresting officer. Second, arrest data can be transferred from officer to computer, from arrest form to arrest form, and from agency to agency, without additional paper or staff. Third and most important, a prisoner can be processed in about 90 minutes.

Table 13-3. *Use of Technology for Arrest Processing in Other Large U.S. Cities* (*N* = 130)

Type of Technology	# of PDs	Percent
Digital Photography	57	43.8%
Digital Fingerprinting	84	64.6%
Data entry of Arrest Information[a]		
PO enters data into car computer	14	10.8%
PO enters data into portable computer	14	10.8%
PO enters data into station house/unspecified computer	14	10.8%
PO may hand-write report or use computer	6	4.6%
Computer Transfer of Arrest Data[a]		
to other arrest forms only	14	10.8%
to other locations /agencies only	16	12.3%
to other forms & other locations	6	4.6%

[a]Some agencies reported more sophisticated technology to transfer arrest-related data, such as barcodes on officer IDs or prisoner wristbands, and integrated processing programs with access to mug shots, prints, rap sheets, arrest documents, etc.

What lessons does the NYPD offer other police agencies? Even if their arrest procedure is half as long as New York's, it still may create problems of overtime cost, loss of patrol strength to processing, and self-interested arrest-seeking and avoidance. And even if processing is brief, it still may lead to some adaptive arrest behavior. A sergeant from an 11-officer agency with a *one-hour* arrest process wrote in an e-mail (6/23/05):

> I could think of instances where I have seen the same behaviors in my guys, as well as committed some of the same myself. Several times I have personally altered arrest decisions based on commitments after work like jobs, family, etc.

Police agencies cannot eliminate the influence of processing on arrest behavior, but they can develop quick, easy procedures by which arrest processing effects are minimized.

RECOMMENDATIONS

UPDATE THE OMNIFORM SYSTEM

A year after the survey was completed, the NYPD introduced the Omniform System. It replaced the antiquated, quirky OLBS with user-friendly, Microsoft-based software. Drop-down menus, check-off boxes, and self-generated serial numbers cut the time needed to prepare Complaint Reports and Arrest Reports. Now officers themselves can complete, print, and save their on-screen Arrest Reports and Complaint Reports with minimum assistance.

But even a casual computer user notices what the Omniform system *cannot* do. It cannot transfer data from one on-screen form to another, so all that duplicate information—officer, perpetrator, victim, time and place of occurrence, and so forth—still has to be rewritten numerous times. The new system fails to incorporate other common arrest paperwork, such as aided cards, lab analysis requests, and property vouchers, so these forms still must be hand-written. The Omniform system cannot electronically transfer Arrest or Complaint Reports to the borough District Attorney, so each document still must be printed out and faxed on unreliable equipment. And while the Omniform System was designed to handle Arrest and Complaint Reports, the department still requires hand-written originals.

A more suitable Omniform System would enable the officer to enter each item of information only once, and have it entered on *every* arrest-related form. Documents could all be stored electronically (no more white originals and pink/yellow/blue/buff copies stuffing department filing cabinets), or sent via computer to the DA's Office.

PROVIDE PORTABLE COMPUTERS
As in other police agencies, NYPD officers should use laptops or computers mounted within patrol cars to directly input arrest-related data from the field. Then, hand-written paperwork could largely be eliminated. The computers, with upgraded Omniform software, could have an attachment to capture complainants' signatures, and could send documents to the station house and district attorney's office. This technology would encourage greater cooperation from complainants, who sometimes decline to prosecute because they dislike spending hours at the police station waiting to sign arrest documents.

HAVE PROCESSING TASKS PERFORMED BY PERSONNEL OTHER THAN THE ARRESTING OFFICERS
Officers in other police agencies turn over their arrests to civilian police employees, county sheriff's deputies, correction officers, or court officers. Then they resume patrol. The NYPD should make greater use of its civilian members to fingerprint and photograph arrestees and assemble case documents. These individuals can be trained to be alert for prisoners' statements and other types of evidence often found during processing. The New York City Department of Corrections should take over prisoner transport, medical screening, escorts to hospitals, and routine custodial care prior to arraignment, because this agency already performs these duties for post-arraignment detainees.

STANDARDIZE ARREST PROCEDURES IN THE FIVE BOROUGHS

Arresting officers should know how to process arrests regardless of the borough of jurisdiction. Presently, each of the five city boroughs imposes its own additional arrest forms, uses its own intake software and procedures, and determines the working hours of its ADAs and arraignment judges. Standardization would both speed processing and assuage the officer's apprehension upon entering a "foreign jurisdiction." This change would require New York City's elected district attorneys and chief administrative judges to treat their respective boroughs as components of a unified system rather than as independent fiefdoms.

HAVE ASSISTANT DISTRICT ATTORNEYS AND ARRAIGNMENT JUDGES WORK THE NIGHT SHIFT

When the ADA and judge go home for the night, arresting officers on the evening shift must interrupt processing, try to catch a half-night's sleep, and resume processing on straight time the next morning. With round-the-clock processing, as is done in some jurisdictions, officers would not be tempted to alter their arrest-making behavior to avoid a tour change. And, continuous processing shortens the time that both prisoners and their keepers are burdened with pre-arraignment custody. (Most detainees are released after arraignment, either though bail, personal recognizance, or a quick guilty plea.)

PROVIDE EXTRA TRAINING ON REPORT WRITING AND TESTIFYING

Two of the most unpleasant aspects of arrest, according to the survey participants, are writing a long, difficult narrative of the incident and giving courtroom testimony. Officers need more report-writing practice and courtroom role-play exercises during recruit and in-service training. With better skills and more confidence, they might be a little less reluctant to arrest.

These six steps would reduce adaptive arrest behavior, because arresting officers would look forward to shorter arrest procedures that afford less profit and less pain. The saving in arrest overtime could defray the costs of these initiatives and perhaps allow officers a basic salary that is more in line with other agencies in the region. However, these suggestions alone would not address other serious post-arrest issues: prisoner detentions and arraignment backlogs. Further changes are needed.

PROVIDE ADEQUATE DETENTION FACILITIES FOR PRISONERS AWAITING ARRAIGNMENT

At Brooklyn Central Booking, where I had supervised the midnight tour, the overcrowded, hazardous accommodations had both human and finan-

cial costs. Because there was only one single body-search station for arriv-
ing prisoners, they and their escorting officers sometimes waited outdoors
in the sally port for hours. Short-staffing or broken cell doors often forced
detainees from three floors levels to squeeze into two. There was barely
enough space in the large holding cells for everyone to sit or lie down, and
if one prisoner inadvertently kicked another or tried to share a cardboard
"mattress," a bloody fight would ensue. Everywhere were mice and water
bugs that would agitate prisoners to the point of near-riots. There was no
freely available drinking water, as the pipes were found to be toxic. The
open toilet bowls, serving up to 50 prisoners apiece, frequently backed up
or overflowed. Disturbances led to injured prisoners and officers, IAB in-
vestigations, and lawsuits against the city.

Because of these conditions, the more vulnerable prisoners had to
remain at the station house, to be guarded one-on-one by a uniformed
officer. Those lodged at Central Booking for twelve hours or more often
required a trip to the emergency room for chest pain, an asthma attack, or
other stress-induced crisis. Even those needing routine medication eventually had to be taken to the hospital just to get a replacement dose, as
they were not permitted to retain their own pharmacy-dispensed medi-
cine. This meant that two uniformed officers from the precinct of arrest
had to go off patrol, drive to Central Booking, transport the prisoner to
the Emergency Room, wait to be seen by medical personnel, and finally
drive the prisoner back.

What would be both humane and economical is a modern holding
area that extends some of the better features of the city correctional system. These include reasonably clean surroundings, on-premises medical
treatment for routine problems, areas to separate vulnerable, infectious,
or disturbed detainees, mats, and reasonable space to lie down, in the
course of a 16-hour stay.

EXPAND COURT CAPACITY

Prisoners who are not arraigned before court closes must remain in police
detention facilities for ten or more additional hours. Aside from keeping
the arraignment courts open, the city should open more community
courts such as the ones in Red Hook, Brooklyn and midtown Manhattan.
Community courts operate on a smaller scale, so they tend to be more innovative and have better case outcomes (*http://www.courtinnovation.org*).
There are a number of city-owned buildings in various boroughs that
could be adapted as local courthouses. This would shorten prisoners' trips
to court and reduce the wait for arraignment. It would also be more con-
venient for complainants.

FINAL COMMENTS

This study was prompted by my observations of how the arrest behavior of fellow officers is affected by arrest processing. This influence has rarely been discussed in police research or included in popular perceptions of the police officer. My survey of 506 officers who regularly perform patrol confirms and quantifies much of what I had witnessed.

The survey indicates that elective arrests are not merely situation-based decisions initiated by chance, but may be planned, managed events. Arrest behavior is affected by overtime concerns, post-work commitments, and arrest-processing burdens. Officers use an array of tactics to control their arrest making in furtherance of self-interest. Their attitudes toward arrest, both cynical and professional, are linked to their arrest behavior. In the context of previously examined arrest determinants, they afford personal arrest factors considerable weight. Finally, officers respond adversely to management attempts to control their arrest behavior through supervision and sanctions.

The survey responses also challenge the general characterizations of police officers as different from everyday folks. The participants are cynical about arrest-making, but they do not appear to be part of an insular subculture alienated from civilian life. Indeed, they would much sooner subordinate their jobs to their personal lives than their personal lives to their jobs. Moreover, the participants are not hardened to affronts to their dignity, security, or physical well-being. In their responses, they disclose very human vulnerabilities.

The principal message for the NYPD is that its arrest-processing procedures are harmful to police officers and to the public, and must be changed. Because of its duration and duress, arrest-making imposes upon the officer an unwanted ethical choice: to be true to the professional values of policing or true to one's own needs and those of one's family. Moreover, protracted processing is costly in terms of overtime dollars and the loss of patrol coverage when officers go out-of-service with an arrest. Finally, the current arrest methods lead to adaptive arrest behavior, which compromises public safety and just execution of the law.

Summary of Findings

In the following review, the most pertinent results of the officer survey are presented under their relevant group or subgroup:

THE CORE SAMPLE

Initially, 655 officers completed the survey. Of these, 506 participants went on patrol at least three times per week, either solo or in two-officer vehicles. Because these officers make the bulk of arrest decisions, they became the main focus of this study as the Core Sample.

DEMOGRAPHICS
- Over 40% of officers live with children or dependent adults whose requirements may compete with those of police work.
- Close to half of officers lack the college credits for promotion, creating a potential conflict between job and school.

ARREST-MAKING ON PATROL
- Almost one-third of officers make no arrests in a typical month, and the overall average is 1.6 arrests per month.
- Officers feel they have ample opportunities to make arrests.
- Close to three quarters of officer patrol with a steady partner, facilitating control of arrest-making.
- Officers postpone arrest-making until the end of the tour, which maximizes overtime.

PRE-INCIDENT PROCLIVITY TO MAKE OR DECLINE ARREST
- Most decisions to arrest, when freely made, are preceded by a pre-tour intent to arrest and by arrest-seeking behaviors.
- Most decisions to decline arrest, if freely made, are preceded by a pre-tour intent to not arrest and by arrest-avoiding behaviors.

FINANCES
- Overtime from routine arrests has become less important than other overtime sources after the attacks of 9/11.
- Officers are "very eager to do better" economically.
- The officer's paycheck is the key financial determinant for most police families: It is 72% of household income overall and is the sole income in one in three households.
- Officers feel their overtime opportunities from sources other than routine arrests to be insufficient.

- While most officers have a moderate need for routine arrest overtime, a distinct segment (18%) rate their need for arrest overtime at the maximum level.
- Officers with greater economic aspirations and fewer structured opportunities for overtime have a higher need for routine arrest overtime money.
- Officers' outside sources of income do not predict their need for routine arrest overtime.

POST-WORK COMMITMENTS

- Because of personal commitments, officers often feel that they cannot extend their tour and, implicitly, cannot make any non-essential arrests.
- Officers with more frequent post-work concerns related to commuting, dependent family members, second jobs, social engagements, other personal business, and school have a more frequent need to end their tour on time.

ARREST-PROCESSING BURDENS

- Officers' most common administrative reasons to dislike arrest-making involve a fear of being humiliated: writing a narrative, testifying in court, and making a mistake, looking bad, or being reprimanded.
- Officers' most common prisoner-related reasons to dislike arrest processing involve a fear not of bodily harm but of verbal risks: Being relentlessly harangued or made subject to an accusation leading to a Civilian Complaint or Internal Affairs investigation.
- Because of arrest-processing difficulties, officers are "turned off" to arrest processing nearly half the time.
- Officers who are more concerned over administrative procedures and dealing with prisoners have a greater aversion to arrest-processing.
- Overall, arrest aversion is more highly associated with administrative processing problems than with prisoner-handling problems.

ARREST-SEEKING AND AVOIDANCE MEASURES

- Officers employ a number of tactics when arrest-seeking for overtime but use them fairly infrequently.
- Officers employ a number of tactics to evade arrest-making, and use them fairly often.
- Officers with a greater need for overtime money also report more frequent use of arrest-seeking adaptations aimed at making overtime.
- Officers with a greater need to end their tour on time also report more frequent use of arrest-avoiding adaptations aimed at timely sign-out.

- Officers with a greater aversion to arrest processing also report more frequent use of adaptations aimed at escaping arrest's procedural burdens.
- Arrest-avoidance measures are more related to sign-out need than to processing aversion.

ATTITUDES TOWARD ARREST

- Officers hold both cynical, self-serving attitudes and positive, professional attitudes toward arrest, but more strongly endorse cynical ones.
- Officers who hold stronger cynical attitudes are slightly inclined to hold weaker professional attitudes.
- Officers believe that their arrests are manipulated to further the careers of prosecutors, commanding officers, and politicians.
- Officers reject claims that their arrests serve professional goals, specifically, that arrests are the mark of a good police officer, that they fulfill public expectations, and that they deter offenders from repeating their crimes.
- Officers strongly oppose the idea that it is all right to arrest a suspect on shaky legal grounds.
- Officers who hold stronger cynical or self-serving attitudes toward arrests engage in more adaptive behaviors aimed at both making overtime and avoiding arrest.
- Officers who hold weaker professional attitudes toward arrest engage in more adaptive arrest behaviors aimed at avoiding arrest; however, their professional attitudes bear no relationship to arrest-seeking for overtime.

PERSONAL CONCERNS IN THE CONTEXT OF OTHER ARREST DETERMINANTS

- Arrest decisions are extremely complex; from a list of 31 arrest factors (16 situational or organizational, and 15 personal), every item carried weight in some participants' decision making.
- Conforming to other studies, the situational factors of offense seriousness, suspect demeanor, and victim cooperation and attitude are the four arrest factors most commonly cited as important.
- Compared to the top four situational variables, the personal arrest factors of post-work social commitments, difficult/dangerous/sick prisoners, and need for overtime money are nearly as important (ranking 5th, 6th, and 8th, respectively).
- Suspect class, race, and gender are rated less important than such personal variables as complicated arrest procedures, being rescheduled, and attending to children.

MANAGERIAL INEFFECTIVENESS

- The patrol supervisor is present just before an arrest is made in one in three incidents and is present when an arrest is declined at one in four. Thus, the supervisor is usually absent at the moment when adaptive arrest behavior can best be discouraged.

- The patrol supervisor overrules subordinates' decisions to *make* an arrest in 7% of incidents and to *decline* arrest in 21% of incidents. Therefore, supervisory reluctance to reverse officer decisions may contribute to adaptive arrest behavior.

- Supervisors intercede more often to order that an arrest be made than to order that an arrest be declined, reflecting officers' greater inclination to resist arrest-making.

- When sanctioned for having too much arrest overtime, officers are more likely to react in ways management did not intend than in ways management intended. Specifically, 51% make no change in behavior, 14% make fewer arrests generally, 12% complain to the union, 6% attempt to make *more* arrests, and 3% put more time into second jobs. Only 10% actually curtailed their cash overtime by either accepting comp time or making fewer end-of-tour arrests.

- When sanctioned for making too few arrests, officers are more likely to react in ways unintended by management than in ways management intended. Specifically, 54% make no behavioral change, 7% complain to the union, 5% "milk" the next arrest for overtime, 3% arrest someone who would ordinarily receive a summons, and 2% try to get a non-patrol assignment. Only 24% of reactions explicitly entailed increased arrest-making, either by making one routine arrest or making just enough arrests to show "average" activity.

NO-ARREST AND HIGH-ARREST OFFICERS IN THE CORE SAMPLE

- From the Core Sample were drawn 151 participants, or 30%, who made no arrests in the last full month they worked, and 94 participants or 19%, who made three or more arrests.

- Finding an arrest is significantly easier for High-Arrest officers than for No-Arrest officers.

- Last-hour arrest-making is more accelerated among the High-Arrest Officers and less accelerated among No-Arrest officers when compared to the Core Sample as a whole.

- No-Arrest and High-Arrest officers are statistically alike in their desire to better themselves financially, in the proportion of their household income coming from non-policing sources, and in the sufficiency of alternative overtime opportunities. These economic circumstances thus appear unrelated to the groups' arrest rates.

- The need for overtime from routine arrests is significantly greater for High-Arrest officers than for No-Arrest officers. Because the High-Arresters and No-Arresters seem to have similar economic circumstances, the High group's perceived need for arrest overtime may stem from a dependency on their overtime-enhanced paychecks once they begin making arrests on a regular basis.
- The need to sign out on time because of outside commitments or concern is significantly greater for No-Arrest officers than for High-Arrest officers.
- Tactics to increase arrest overtime are used significantly more by High-Arrest officers than by No-Arrest officers.
- Tactics to avoid arrest, for both timely sign-out and processing aversion, are used significantly more by No-Arrest officers than by High-Arrest officers.
- The prospect of prisoner difficulties is the most important personal arrest variable for No-Arrest officers.
- The prospect of overtime is the most important personal arrest variable for High-Arrest officers.
- The No-Arrest group gives much greater weight in its arrest decisions to concerns over complicated processing procedures and the need to attend to children than the High-Arrest group does.
- The High-Arrest group gives much greater weight in arrest decisions to concerns over career advancement or plainclothes assignment than the No-Arrest groups.
- No-Arrest and High-Arrest officers are equally cynical about arrest-making, but the High-Arresters alone subscribe to the professional attitudes that arrests are the mark of a good police officer and that minor arrests deter more serious crime.

MALE AND FEMALE OFFICERS IN THE CORE SAMPLE

- Female officers are given patrol assignments significantly less often than males. Only 71% percent of female officers, as compared to 90% of men, met the Core Sample criterion of three or more patrol days per week. From the Core Sample, the 379 males and 68 females who reported their gender, respectively, represent valid percentages of 85% and 15%.
- Thirty-two percent of female officers, as opposed to only 4% of male officers, are raising children without a spouse or partner.
- Female and male officers make a statistically equivalent number of arrests.

- Female officers have significantly more family-related time commitments than male officers.
- Female and male officers have the same overall need to get off work on time, perhaps because they share a number of "gender-neutral" time constraints like commuting difficulties. It is also possible that the women officers with greater family-related time constraints gravitate to the non-Core group, which is disproportionately female.
- Female and male officers use adaptive arrest tactics—both to seek and avoid arrest—at statistically similar rates.

TOUR: MIDNIGHTS, DAYS, AND EVENINGS

- Of the Core Sample, 88 officers, or 17.6%, were assigned to the midnight tour, 173 or 34.7% to days, and 171 or 34.3% to evenings. Tour was thought to be a possible factor in adaptive arrest behavior because the anomic working conditions of midnight tours may be conducive to police misconduct and because arrests on midnight tours potentially afford the most overtime.
- Arrest rates among the midnight, day, and evening tours are approximately equal.
- Officers on the three tours are alike in how often they engaged in arrest-seeking tactics aimed at overtime.
- Officers on the three tours are alike in how often they engaged in arrest-avoidance tactics aimed at timely sign-out and avoidance of processing.

CONTRASTING BOROUGHS: QUEENS AND THE BRONX

- Of the Core Sample, 123 officers, or 19%, work in Queens, where crime rates are relatively low and arrest processing time is the quickest of any borough. One-hundred and ten officers, or 17%, work in the Bronx, where crime rates are sharply higher, and arrest processing is nearly three hours longer.
- Bronx officers average 2.1 arrests in the previous month, nearly twice as the 1.2 arrests made by Queens officers.
- Bronx officers use arrest-seeking adaptations significantly more than do officers from Queens.
- The Bronx officers may be reacting to not only the financial rewards of protracted processing but to a norm of frequent arrest-making in precincts with serious crime.

- Despite their longer and more arduous processing, Bronx officers are no more "turned off" to arrest processing than are Queens officers, nor do they use more arrest-avoiding adaptations. Bronx officers may more accepting of processing burdens as a necessary evil in fighting crime, and/or they may perceive their ten hours of processing as not that much worse than the seven hours endured by their Queens counterparts.

Survey of Patrol Officers

JOHN JAY COLLEGE OF CRIMINAL JUSTICE

The City University of New York
899 Tenth Avenue, New York, N.Y. 10019
(212) 237-8000

Information for Participants in this Study

My name is Edith Linn and I am a lieutenant in the Queens Court Section. Through John Jay College and the CUNY Graduate Center, I am working on a doctoral dissertation about personal factors in arrest discretion. Its aim is to increase our understanding of how concerns like financial need, time constraints, and feelings toward arrest processing may influence arrest decisions. Although the Department has granted me its permission, THIS STUDY IS NOT INITIATED OR CONTROLLED BY THE NYPD.

I have prepared the following <u>voluntary</u>, <u>anonymous</u> questionnaire for distribution to approximately 500 officers who routinely perform patrol. Though the survey appears long, it takes officers only about thirty-five minutes to finish. You may decline to answer a question or cease participation at any time, without penalty. But to achieve a valid result, I ask that you answer each item as accurately as possible, based on your own situation and perspective.

Some of the items may seem personal or sensitive. To assure your anonymity, the questions are structured so as to make it impossible to identify any specific officer. Moreover, you will be sealing the questionnaire in its envelope, and returning it in random order. If the results of the study are published, the anonymity of all participants will be maintained.

The ultimate goal of this research is to find ways to ease the conflicts between officers' professional duties and their personal lives. If you would like to learn the final results of the study, you can reach me at John Jay College Ph.D. Program in Criminal Justice, 899 Tenth Avenue #434, New York, NY 10019, (212) 237-8419, or through e-mail at <u>edie188@aol.com.</u> (You need not identify yourself when contacting me, unless you chose to.) Inquiries may also be directed to Dr. Ned Benton, Dissertation Advisor, at (212) 237-8070 or nbenton@faculty.jjay.cuny.edu. If you have questions about your rights as a participant in the study, you can contact Hilry Fisher, Sponsored Research, the Graduate Center, (212) 817-7523 or hfisher@gc.cuny.edu.

Thank you for your contribution to this research.

1. How long have you been a police officer? *(Write one number, for example, 0 2, per line)*
   __ __ years & __ __ months

2. About how long have you been assigned to your present command?
   (Write one number per line) __ ___years & __ __ months

3. How would you describe the overall crime rate in the area you patrol?
   (Circle a number along scale.)
   Very Low   **0......1......2......3......4......5......6......7......,8.,....9......10**   Very High

4. What is your usual tour? *(Circle letter.)*
   A. 1st Platoon (12x8)   **B.** 2nd Platoon (8x4)   **C.** 3rd Platoon (4x12)   **D.** Scooter Chart
   E. Other *(Describe)* _____

5. How often are you assigned to go out on patrol? *(Circle letter.)*
   A. Never/Very Rarely   **B.** 1–4 times/month   **C.** 1 in 5 tours   **D.** 2 in 5 tours   **E.** 3 in 5 tours
   F. 4 in 5 tours   **G.** Almost every tour

6. Please write in each space what assignments you might have in a typical five-day set
   (e.g., sector car, SP10, foot post, TS, etc):
   day 1 _____day 2 _____day 3 _____day 4 _____ day 5 _____

7. In a typical week, how many tours do you work with the same partner? *(Circle letter.)*
   A. 5   **B.** 4   **C.** 3   **D.** 2   **E.** fewer than 2

8. How hard or easy is it to find an arrest while patrolling in your command?
   (Circle a number along scale.)
   usually very easy   **0....1....2....3....4....5....6....7....8....9....10**   usually very hard
   to find an arrest   to find an arrest

9. What was the most recent month when you worked, full-duty, for at least <u>3 weeks</u> **or**
   <u>15 tours</u>? *(Write month.)* _____

10. How many<u> arrests</u>, if any, did you make in that month? *(Write one number per line.)*
    ____ ____

11. How many <u>arrests</u>, if any, did you assist a <u>partner</u> in making in that month?
    (Write one number per line.) ____ ____

12. How many <u>hours of overtime</u>, if any, did you earn from arrests made <u>on routine
    patrol</u> in that month? *(Write one number per line.)* ____ ____

13. About how many hours of <u>overtime</u>, if any, did you earn in <u>special enforcement
    assignments</u> that may generate arrests or summonses (e.g., CONDOR,
    Red-light overtime) in that month? *(Write one number per line.)* ____ ____

14. About how many <u>hours of non-arrest/non-enforcement overtime</u> (e.g., WTC/ security posts/special events) did you earn in that month? *(Write one number per line.)* ____ ____

15. How do your <u>arrest numbers</u> compare to officers with similar assignments in your unit? *(Circle number on scale.)*
Well below average **0**…..**1**…..**2**…..**3**…..**4**…..**5**…..**6**…..**7**…..**8**…..**9**…..**10** Well above average

16. How does your <u>arrest overtime</u> compare to officers with similar assignments in your unit? *(Circle number on scale.)*
Well below average **0**…..**1**…..**2**…..**3**…..**4**…..**5**…..**6**…..**7**…..**8**…..**9**…..**10** Well above average

17. About what percent of overtime, if any, do you usually take in <u>time</u> rather than cash? *(Circle percentage.)*
0%……**10%**……**20%**……**30%**……**40%**……**50%**……**60%**……**70%**……**80%**……**90%**……**100%**

18. About what portion of your arrests, if any, are made in <u>the **second half** of your tour</u>? *(Circle percentage.)*
0%……**10%**……**20%**……**30%**……**40%**……**50%**……**60%**……**70%**……**80%**……**90%**……**100%**

19. About what portion of your arrests, if any, are made in <u>the last **hour** of your tour</u>? *(Circle percentage.)*
0%……**10%**……**20%**……**30%**……**40%**……**50%**……**60%**……**70%**……**80%**……**90%**……**100%**

20. How do you feel about your <u>present ability to afford the things you want</u>? *(Circle number on scale.)*
Very able right now **0**…..**1**…..**2**…..**3**…..**4**…..**5**…..**6**…..**7**…..**8**…..**9**…..**10** Very eager to do better

21. What percent of your total household income comes from <u>sources **other than** your police salary</u>, like a spouse's salary, second job, rental income, government subsidy, military service, rich parents, etc.? *(Circle percentage.)*
0%……**10%**……**20%**……**30%**……**40%**……**50%**……**60%**……**70%**……**80%**……**90%**……**100%**

22. How would you describe your present <u>opportunities to earn overtime by means **other than** through arrest-making on routine patrol</u> (i.e., any other overtime source—special events, CONDOR, WTC, etc.)? *(Circle number on scale.)*
Never enough **0**…..**1**…..**2**…..**3**…..**4**…..**5**…..**6**…..**7**…..**8**…..**9**…..**10** More than enough

23. To what extent do you <u>**need** overtime money from arrests made on **routine patrol**</u>? *(Circle number on scale.)*
Never any real need **0**…..**1**…..**2**…..**3**…..**4**…..**5**…..**6**…..**7**…..**8**…..**9**…..**10** Always a great need

24. About how often do you have to take care of <u>children or dependent family members</u> …in general? *(Circle letter.)*
A. Rarely/Never   B. 1–4 days/month   C. 1 day/week   D. 2 days/week   E. 3 days/week
F. 4 days/week G. 5 or more days/week

…within three hours after your tour? *(Circle letter.)*
A. Rarely/Never   B. 1–4 days/month   C. 1 day/week   D. 2 days/week   E. 3 days/week   F. 4 days/week G. 5 or more days/week

25. About how often do you attend <u>school</u> or prepare school assignments…in general? *(Circle letter.)*
A. Rarely/Never   B. 1—4 days/month   C. 1 day/week   D. 2 days/week   E. 3 days/week F. 4 days/week G. 5 or more days/week
…within three hours after your tour? *(Circle letter.)*
A. Rarely/Never   B. 1–4 days/month   C. 1 day/week   D. 2 days/week   E. 3 days/week F. 4 days/week G. 5 or more days/week

26. About how often do you go to a <u>second job</u> (even "off-the-record")…in general? *(Circle letter.)*
A. Rarely/Never   B. 1–4 days/month   C. 1 day/week   D. 2 days/week   E. 3 days/week F. 4 days/week G. 5 or more days/week
…within three hours after your tour? *(Circle letter.)*
A. Rarely/Never   B. 1–4 days/month   C. 1 day/week   D. 2 days/week   E. 3 days/week F. 4 days/week G. 5 or more days/week

27. About how often do you have <u>social commitments</u>, such as sports teams, fraternal organizations, family gatherings, dates, etc. …in general? *(Circle letter.)*
A. Rarely/Never   B. 1–4 days/month   C. 1 day/week   D. 2 days/week   E. 3 days/week F. 4 days/week G. 5 or more days/week
…within three hours after your tour? *(Circle letter.)*
A. Rarely/Never   B. 1–4 days/month   C. 1 day/week   D. 2 days/week   E. 3 days/week F. 4 days/week G. 5 or more days/week

28. About how often do you have <u>other personal commitments or appointments</u>, aside from those above…in general? *(Circle letter.)*
A. Rarely/Never   B. 1–4 days/month   C. 1 day/week   D. 2 days/week   E. 3 days/week F. 4 days/week G. 5 or more days/week
…within three hours after your tour? *(Circle letter.)*
A. Rarely/Never   B. 1–4 days/month   C. 1 day/week   D. 2 days/week   E. 3 days/week F. 4 days/week G. 5 or more days/week

29. Do you have any of the following <u>commuting concerns</u> when leaving work? *(Circle letter or letters.)*
A. a car pool   **B**. beating rush hour   **C**. catching train/bus/ferry   **D**. other *(describe)* _____

30. About <u>how often</u> do you have commuting concerns when leaving work?
(Circle letter.)
A. Rarely/Never   **B.** 1–4 days/month   **C.** 1 day/week   **D.** 2 days/week
E. 3 days/week   **F.** 4 days/week   **G.** 5 or more days/week

31. Overall, about how often do you feel you <u>must end your tour on time</u> because of
one or more of the above commitments or concerns?   *(Circle letter.)*
A. Rarely/Never   **B.** 1–4 days/month   **C.** 1 day/week   **D.** 2 days/week
E. 3 days/week   **F.** 4 days/week   **G.** 5 or more days/week

32. Below are aspects of the arrest-making's <u>administrative procedures</u> that may be
unpleasant or risky. Please indicate the degree to which each item is a concern for
<u>you</u>. *(Place check in selected column.)*

Never a concern	**Rarely** a concern	**Sometimes** a concern	**Often** a concern	**Always** a concern

a. Procedures are tiring, especially after working 8 hours.

_____   _____   _____   _____   _____

b. Arrest forms are boring and repetitious.

_____   _____   _____   _____   _____

c. Procedures may be complex or confusing.

_____   _____   _____   _____   _____

d. May need to write lengthy or difficult narrative.

_____   _____   _____   _____   _____

e. May need to go to different locations (e.g., DWI).

_____   _____   _____   _____   _____

f. May need to testify.

_____   _____   _____   _____   _____

g. May make mistake/ look bad / be reprimanded.

_____   _____   _____   _____   _____

h. May be disciplined for taking too long.

_____   _____   _____   _____   _____

i. Computer / other processing equipment may be down.

_____   _____   _____   _____   _____

j. Staff with computer/equipment skills may be unavailable.

_____   _____   _____   _____   _____

k. Other administrative problems? *(describe)*

_____

_____

_____

33. Below are aspects of <u>handling arrested persons</u> that may be unpleasant or risky.
Please indicate the degree to which each item is a concern for <u>you.</u>
(Place check in selected column.)

Never a concern	**Rarely** a concern	**Sometimes** a concern	**Often** a concern	**Always** a concern

a. Prisoner may be violent.

_____   _____   _____   _____   _____

b. Prisoner may be verbally abusive.

_____   _____   _____   _____   _____

c. Prisoner may be EDP/drunk.

_____   _____   _____   _____   _____

d. Prisoner may be infectious (AIDS, TB, lice, etc.)

_____   _____   _____   _____   _____

e. Prisoner may be filthy, have foul odor.

_____   _____   _____   _____   _____

f. Prisoner may need to go to hospital.

_____   _____   _____   _____   _____

g. Prisoner may try to escape.

_____   _____   _____   _____   _____

h. Prisoner may make allegations (CCRB, IAB, etc.)

_____   _____   _____   _____   _____

i. Other prisoner problems? *(describe)*

_____

_____

_____

34. How often are you <u>seriously **"turned off"** to making an arrest</u> because of its actual
or potential discomforts and risks (stemming from either administrative and/or
prisoner-handling factors)? *(Circle number on scale.)*

On no occasion **0**…..**1**…..**2**…..**3**…..**4**…..**5**…..**6**…..**7**…..**8**…..**9**…..**10** On every occasion
half the
time

35. Below are methods officers might use to increase their arrest overtime. Please indicate the extent to which you may have used each method for the purpose of increasing arrest overtime *(Place check in selected column)*.

Never	**Rarely**	**Sometimes**	**Often**	**Always**

a. Switched to assignment with good arrest opportunities

———————   ———————   ———————   ———————   ———————

b. Asked officers for their unwanted arrests

———————   ———————   ———————   ———————   ———————

c. Made more MDT checks and/or car stops in 2nd half of tour

———————   ———————   ———————   ———————   ———————

d. Made more Stop/Question/Frisks in 2nd half of tour

———————   ———————   ———————   ———————   ———————

e. Patrolled in areas known for easy arrests in 2nd half of tour

———————   ———————   ———————   ———————   ———————

f. Tried to arrive faster at crimes in progress in 2nd half of tour

———————   ———————   ———————   ———————   ———————

g. Tried hard to find suspects who left scene in 2nd half of tour

———————   ———————   ———————   ———————   ———————

h. Tried to take domestic incident jobs in 2nd half of tour

———————   ———————   ———————   ———————   ———————

i. Tried harder to get complainants to prosecute in 2nd half of tour

———————   ———————   ———————   ———————   ———————

j. Tried to handle jobs before alerting dispatcher in 2nd half of tour

———————   ———————   ———————   ———————   ———————

k. Issued a DAT instead of a summons in 2nd half of tour

———————   ———————   ———————   ———————   ———————

l. Looked for any minor violation in 2nd half of tour

———————   ———————   ———————   ———————   ———————

m. Followed up on every pick-up complaint in 2nd half of tour

———————   ———————   ———————   ———————   ———————

n. Focused more on minority individuals who might be perps

———————   ———————   ———————   ———————   ———————

o. Other methods you used *(describe)*.

_____

_____

_____

36. How often <u>overall</u> do you take measures like those above to make arrests <u>because</u>
<u>you need overtime money</u>? *(Circle letter.)*
A. Rarely /Never   **B.** 1–4 times/month   **C.** Once/week   **D.** Twice/week
E. 3 times /week   **F.** 4 times/week **G.** every tour

37. Below are methods officers might use to <u>avoid making arrests.</u> Please indicate the
extent to which <u>you</u> may have used **each** method in order to <u>get off work on time</u>,
and/or <u>avoid the discomforts and risks of arrest-processing</u> .
(Place check in selected column.)

Never   **Rarely**   **Sometimes**   **Often**   **Always**

a. Arranged to get assignment having little or no chance to arrest

——————   ——————   ——————   ——————   ——————

b. Asked fellow officers to take any arrest you may get stuck with

——————   ——————   ——————   ——————   ——————

c. Made few or no RMP computer checks / car stops

——————   ——————   ——————   ——————   ——————

d. Conducted few or no Stop/Question/Frisks

——————   ——————   ——————   ——————   ——————

e. Avoided patrol areas where arrests "fall into your lap"

——————   ——————   ——————   ——————   ——————

f. Drove slowly or conspicuously (lights, sirens) to crimes in progress

——————   ——————   ——————   ——————   ——————

g. Avoided assignments to domestic incidents

——————   ——————   ——————   ——————   ——————

h. Tried to discourage complainants from pressing charges

——————   ——————   ——————   ——————   ——————

i. Tried to dispose of jobs without alerting dispatcher/supervisor

——————   ——————   ——————   ——————   ——————

j. Issued a summons instead of making an arrest

——————   ——————   ——————   ——————   ——————

k. Ignored minor violations (e.g., drinking /urinating /smoking weed)

——————   ——————   ——————   ——————   ——————

l. Ignored pick-up complaints from non-involved parties

——————   ——————   ——————   ——————   ——————

n. Other methods you used *(describe).*

_____

_____

_____

38. About how often <u>overall</u> do you take measures to avoid arrests like those above because you need to<u> get off work on time</u>? *(Circle letter.)*

A. Rarely/Never   **B**. 1–4 times/month   **C**. Once/week   **D**. Twice/week
E. 3 times/week   **F**. 4 times/week   **G**. Every tour

39. About how often <u>overall</u> do you take measures to avoid arrests like those above because of the<u> risks / discomforts of</u> <u>administrative procedures or handling of prisoners</u>? *(Circle letter.)*

A. Rarely/Never   **B**. 1–4 times/month   **C**. Once/week   **D**. Twice/week
E. 3 times/week   **F**. 4 times/week   **G**. Every tour

40. Below are factors officers may weigh while on routine patrol when faced with a possible arrest situation. Please indicate how often these factors are important in <u>your own</u> decisions to arrest or not arrest while on routine patrol.
(Place check in selected column.)

Never	**Rarely**	**Sometimes**	**Often**	**Always**
a. level/seriousness of the offense				
_____	_____	_____	_____	_____
b. class/type of suspect (derelict, blue-collar, VIP, etc.)				
_____	_____	_____	_____	_____
c. pedigree of suspect (race, sex, age, etc.)				
_____	_____	_____	_____	_____
d. attitude/demeanor of the suspect				
_____	_____	_____	_____	_____
e. class of complainant/victim (homeless, blue-collar, VIP, etc.)				
_____	_____	_____	_____	_____
f. pedigree of complainant/victim (race, sex, age, etc.)				
_____	_____	_____	_____	_____
g. attitude/demeanor of complainant/victim				
_____	_____	_____	_____	_____
h. willingness of complainant to prosecute				
_____	_____	_____	_____	_____
i. desires/expectations of community				
_____	_____	_____	_____	_____
j. pressure from supervisor/C.O. to make arrest				
_____	_____	_____	_____	_____
k. need to make overtime money				
_____	_____	_____	_____	_____
l. need to make comp time				
_____	_____	_____	_____	_____

m. pressure to limit overtime

_____   _____   _____   _____   _____

n. need to get off work on time for child-related activity

_____   _____   _____   _____   _____

o. need to get off work on time for college-related activity

_____   _____   _____   _____   _____

p. need to get off work on time for second job

_____   _____   _____   _____   _____

q. need to get off work on time for social commitment

_____   _____   _____   _____   _____

r. need to carpool/beat rush hour/catch train, etc.

_____   _____   _____   _____   _____

s. likeliness of being rescheduled to see ADA/go to court

_____   _____   _____   _____   _____

t. desire for career advancement / plainclothes assignment

_____   _____   _____   _____   _____

u. desire to go into station house / take a break from patrol

_____   _____   _____   _____   _____

v. bad weather

_____   _____   _____   _____   _____

w. boredom

_____   _____   _____   _____   _____

x. long/complicated paperwork or processing

_____   _____   _____   _____   _____

y. difficult / dangerous / filthy / sick prisoner

_____   _____   _____   _____   _____

z. request to take coworker's arrest / give away your arrest

_____   _____   _____   _____   _____

aa. lack of another officer to take your arrest

_____   _____   _____   _____   _____

bb. manpower / number of sectors running

_____   _____   _____   _____   _____

cc. judgment /opinions of other officers

_____   _____   _____   _____   _____

dd. presence of supervisor

_____   _____   _____   _____   _____

ee. presence of bystanders / personal safety

_____   _____   _____   _____   _____

ff. other _____

_____

_____

The next group of questions (41–48) concerns the **most recent arrest** you made in the course of routine patrol, <u>within the last **three**</u> months.
(Please write "N/A"–not applicable–if you have <u>not</u> processed an arrest in the last three months):

41. About how many <u>days</u> ago was the arrest? *(Write one number per line)* ____ ____

42. What was the offense or offenses involved? _____

43. Was a supervisor present from the beginning of the incident? *(Circle.)* **Yes / No**

44. Was the arrest procedurally mandated or otherwise unavoidable (e.g., Domestic Violence, Security Holding, Serious Crime, Patrol Supervisor's order, etc.)?
(Circle.) **Yes / No**
If "**Yes**," please explain. _____

45. At the <u>beginning</u> of your tour, to what extent did you <u>want</u> to make an arrest?
(Circle number on scale.)
Strongly <u>didn't</u> want **0....1....2....3....4....5....6....7....8....9....10** Strongly <u>wanted</u>
    an arrest   an arrest
                      no preference

46. Before the possible arrest situation arose, how would you describe your <u>patrol activities</u>? *(Circle number on scale.)*
Trying hard to <u>avoid</u> **0....1....2....3....4....5....6....7....8....9....10** Trying hard to
    an arrest   <u>make</u> an arrest
               neither seeking nor avoiding arrest

47. How did you <u>get involved</u> in the arrest situation? *(Circle letter.)*
a. Pursuant to self-initiated investigative/enforcement activity (car stop, stop/question/frisk, etc.)
b. The primary unit didn't want the arrest and you offered to take it
c. Dispatcher announced job and you/your partner offered to take it
d. Pick-up job – approached by non-involved witness
e. Pick-up job – approached by complainant
f. Dispatcher/TS assigned you the job
g. Supervisor made you take arrest
h. Other *(Describe.)* _____

48. If this arrest was NOT mandatory or unavoidable (i.e., you answered "**No**" to # 44), to what extent did the following factors affect you in making **this particular arrest decision** *(Place a check in selected column)*:

not a factor	**minor factor**	**moderate factor**	**major factor**

a. level of offense

_____	_____	_____	_____

b. suspect attitude/demeanor

_____	_____	_____	_____

c. other suspect trait (class, age, gender, race, etc.)

_____   _____   _____   _____

d. complainant cooperation/attitude

_____   _____   _____   _____

e. complaint trait (class, age, gender, race, etc.)

_____   _____   _____   _____

f. need for overtime cash/time

_____   _____   _____   _____

g. pressure to arrest from supervisor/C.O.

_____   _____   _____   _____

h. lousy day on patrol (boredom, bad weather, etc.)

_____   _____   _____   _____

i. opinion of fellow officers/lack of another available A/O

_____   _____   _____   _____

j. desires/expectations of community

_____   _____   _____   _____

k. presence of bystanders /personal safety

_____   _____   _____   _____

l. desire for career advancement/plainclothes assignment

_____   _____   _____   _____

m. other *(describe)*

_____

_____

_____

The next group of questions (49–55) concerns the **most recent time**, within the last **three** months, that you **DECLINED a possible arrest** while on routine patrol and no other officer took the arrest, i.e., it was "shitcanned." *(Please write "N/A" – not applicable - if you have not been in this situation within the last three months.)*

49. About how many days ago was this opportunity for an arrest ? *(Write one number per line)* ____ ____

50. What was the offense or offenses in question? _____

51. Was a supervisor present at the scene? *(Circle.)* **Yes / No**

52. At the beginning of your tour on the day this arrest was declined, to what extent did you want to make an arrest?
Strongly didn't want **0....1....2....3....4....5....6....7....8....9....10** Strongly wanted
an arrest   an arrest
no preference

53. Before the possible arrest situation arose, how would you describe your
patrol activities?
Trying hard to avoid **0....1....2....3....4....5....6....7....8....9....10** Trying hard to
      an arrest   make an arrest
                          neither seeking nor avoiding arrest

54. How did you get involved in the situation in which you ultimately declined the
arrest? *(Circle letter.)*
a. Pursuant to self-initiated investigative/enforcement activity (car stop,
stop/question/frisk, etc.)
b. Dispatcher announced job and you/your partner offered to take it
c. Pick-up job – approached by non-involved witness
d. Pick-up job – approached by complainant
e. Dispatcher/TS assigned you to back up the job
f. Supervisor directed you to the job
g. Other _____

55. To what extent did the following factors affect you in making **this particular
decision** to **decline** this arrest?
*(Place check in selected column)***:**

not a factor	minor factor	moderate factor	major factor
a. level of offense			
____	____	____	____
b. suspect attitude/demeanor			
____	____	____	____
c. other suspect trait (class, age, gender, race, etc.)			
____	____	____	____
d. complainant cooperation/attitude			
____	____	____	____
e. complaint trait (class, age, gender, race, etc.)			
____	____	____	____
f. need for overtime cash/time			
____	____	____	____
g. pressure to arrest from supervisor/C.O.			
____	____	____	____
h. lousy day on patrol (boredom, bad weather, etc.)			
____	____	____	____
i. opinion of fellow officers/lack of another available A/O			
____	____	____	____
j. desires/expectations of community			
____	____	____	____
k. presence of bystanders /personal safety			
____	____	____	____

l. other *(describe)*

_____

_____

_____

56. Below are 15 statements. Each is followed by an opinion scale, wherein "0" indicates the strongest disagreement, "5" indicates a neutral position, and "10" indicates the strongest agreement. Please indicate the extent to which you agree or disagree with each statement along its scale. *(Circle number.)*

a. "Making good arrests is a way for officers to advance in their career."
Strongly <u>disagree</u> **0**.....**1**.....**2**.....**3**.....**4**.....**5**.....**6**.....**7**.....**8**.....**9**.....**10** Strongly <u>agree</u>
                                            neutral

b. "Arrests deter offenders from repeating their criminal behavior."
Strongly <u>disagree</u> **0**.....**1**.....**2**.....**3**.....**4**.....**5**.....**6**.....**7**.....**8**.....**9**.....**10** Strongly <u>agree</u>
                                            neutral

c. "Arrest statistics are manipulated by the C.O. or higher brass to make themselves look good."
Strongly <u>disagree</u> **0**.....**1**.....**2**.....**3**.....**4**.....**5**.....**6**.....**7**.....**8**.....**9**.....**10** Strongly <u>agree</u>
                                            neutral

d. "Arrest policies depend more on 'politics' than on concepts of sound crime-fighting."
Strongly <u>disagree</u> **0**.....**1**.....**2**.....**3**.....**4**.....**5**.....**6**.....**7**.....**8**.....**9**.....**10** Strongly <u>agree</u>
                                            neutral

e. "Arrests for "quality of life" offenses prevent more serious crime problems."
Strongly <u>disagree</u> **0**.....**1**.....**2**.....**3**.....**4**.....**5**.....**6**.....**7**.....**8**.....**9**.....**10** Strongly <u>agree</u>
                                            neutral

f. "ADAs will plea bargain a felony to a violation if it means an easy conviction."
Strongly <u>disagree</u> **0**.....**1**.....**2**.....**3**.....**4**.....**5**.....**6**.....**7**.....**8**.....**9**.....**10** Strongly <u>agree</u>
                                            neutral

g. "Arrests represent the way society enforces basic standards of right and wrong."
Strongly <u>disagree</u> **0**.....**1**.....**2**.....**3**.....**4**.....**5**.....**6**.....**7**.....**8**.....**9**.....**10** Strongly <u>agree</u>
                                            neutral

h. "Making arrests isn't worth it if they really disrupt your home life."
Strongly <u>disagree</u> **0**.....**1**.....**2**.....**3**.....**4**.....**5**.....**6**.....**7**.....**8**.....**9**.....**10** Strongly <u>agree</u>
                                            neutral

i. "Arresting on shaky legal grounds is o.k. if you figure that the perp got away with many other crimes."
Strongly <u>disagree</u> **0**.....**1**.....**2**.....**3**.....**4**.....**5**.....**6**.....**7**.....**8**.....**9**.....**10** Strongly <u>agree</u>
                                            neutral

j. "A good police officer should regularly make arrests."
Strongly <u>disagree</u> **0**.....**1**.....**2**.....**3**.....**4**.....**5**.....**6**.....**7**.....**8**.....**9**.....**10** Strongly <u>agree</u>
                                            neutral

k. "Judges will accept almost any plea bargain just to clear their calendars."
Strongly <u>disagree</u> **0**.....**1**.....**2**.....**3**.....**4**.....**5**.....**6**.....**7**.....**8**.....**9**.....**10** Strongly <u>agree</u>
                                            neutral

l. "No arrest is worth risking serious injury."
Strongly <u>disagree</u> **0**.....**1**.....**2**.....**3**.....**4**.....**5**.....**6**.....**7**.....**8**.....**9**.....**10** Strongly <u>agree</u>
neutral

m. "It's no big deal if a perp gets away, as he'll get caught sooner or later doing something else."
Strongly <u>disagree</u> **0**.....**1**.....**2**.....**3**.....**4**.....**5**.....**6**.....**7**.....**8**.....**9**.....**10** Strongly <u>agree</u>
neutral

n. "Arrests show that the police are doing what the what the public expects of them."
Strongly <u>disagree</u> **0**.....**1**.....**2**.....**3**.....**4**.....**5**.....**6**.....**7**.....**8**.....**9**.....**10** Strongly <u>agree</u>
neutral

o. "A person who takes the oath of a police officer should be prepared to make sacrifices."
Strongly <u>disagree</u> **0**.....**1**.....**2**.....**3**.....**4**.....**5**.....**6**.....**7**.....**8**.....**9**.....**10** Strongly <u>agree</u>
neutral

The next set of items concern supervisors' involvement in your arrest decisions. Please complete them based your own experience.

57. *(Skip this item if you made no arrests in the past three months.)*
About what percent of the time (if at all) has the patrol supervisor arrived at an arrest incident <u>before</u> you placed the individual under arrest? *(Circle percentage.)*

0%.....**10%**.....**20%**.....**30%**.....**40%**.....**50%**.....**60%**.....**70%**.....**80%**.....**90%**.....**100%**
never   half the time   every time

58. *(Skip this item if you have not <u>declined</u> an arrest in the past three months.)*
About what percent of the time (if at all) is the patrol supervisor at the scene when you have <u>not</u> made an arrest that you could have made? *(Circle percentage.)*

0%.....**10%**.....**20%**.....**30%**.....**40%**.....**50%**.....**60%**.....**70%**.....**80%**.....**90%**.....**100%**
never   half the time   every time

59. About what percent of the time (if at all) has a patrol supervisor at an incident told you <u>not</u> to make an arrest you wanted to make? *(Circle percentage.)*
0%.....**10%**.....**20%**.....**30%**.....**40%**.....**50%**.....**60%**.....**70%**.....**80%**.....**90%**.....**100%**
never   half the time   every time

60. About what percent of the time (if at all) has a patrol supervisor at an incident ordered you to make an arrest that you did not want to make? *(Circle percentage.)*
0%.....**10%**.....**20%**.....**30%**.....**40%**.....**50%**.....**60%**.....**70%**.....**80%**.....**90%**.....**100%**
never   half the time   every time

61. How much time are you allowed to complete arrest paperwork and get a "Police-Ready" time? _____ hours.

62. How adequate is the time allowed for you to complete arrest processing? *(Circle number on scale.)*
Never enough **0.....1.....2.....3.....4.....5.....6.....7.....8.....9.....10** Always enough

63. How <u>strict</u> is your command about going past arrest-processing time limits and incurring extra overtime? *(Circle number on scale.)*
not at all strict,   very strict,
  any reason ok, **0......1......2......3......4......5......6......7......8......9......10** no excuses,
  no penalty   likely CD

64. How often, if ever, has a supervisor reassigned an arrest that you made late in your tour to another officer? *(Circle number on scale.)*
never **0.......1.......2......3......4... ....5......6.......7.......8.......9.......10** very often

65. How often, if ever, has a supervisor reassigned a late-in-tour arrest made by another officer to <u>you?</u> *(Circle number on scale.)*
never **0.......1.......2......3......4... ....5......6.......7.......8.......9.......10** very often

66. How often, if ever, has a supervisor's reassignment of another officer's arrest <u>to you</u> caused you a problem in preparing paperwork, answering the ADA's questions, testifying, etc.?
never **0.......1.......2......3......4... ....5......6.......7.......8.......9.......10** very often
Please describe any problem(s) you may have had: _____

_____

67. How often, if ever, have you and another officer arranged to have the other officer take <u>your</u> arrest? *(Circle number on scale.)*
never **0.......1.......2......3......4... ....5......6.......7.......8.......9.......10** very often

68. How often, if ever, have you and another officer arranged to have you take the <u>other officer's arrest?</u> *(Circle number on scale.)*
never **0.......1.......2......3......4... ....5......6.......7.......8.......9.......10** very often

69. How often, if ever, has an arrangement with a fellow officer to take the other officer's arrest, caused you a problem in preparing paperwork, answering the ADA's questions, testifying, etc.?
never **0.......1.......2......3......4... ....5......6.......7.......8.......9.......10** very often
Please describe any problem(s) you may have had: _____

_____

70. In the past 12 months, about how many times, if at all, did you earn more overtime than management would like? *(Circle.)*
Never   1 time   **2** times   **3** times   4 times   **5** times   6 times
7 times   8 times   **9** times   **10** times   **12** times

(If in the last 12 months you <u>never</u> earned more overtime than management would like, write "N/A"- not applicable - over the rest of this page.)

71. The following is a list of consequences that police management may threaten, or actually impose, for making too much cash overtime. Below, to the right, is a list of ways officers may react to their bosses' actions.

In the first list, please indicate any consequence(s) <u>you</u> experienced. *(Circle the letter.)*

Then, from the list at the bottom, indicate <u>your</u> reaction(s) to each consequence you experienced. *(Write the number of up to four different reactions for each consequence you circled in the blank lines that follow.)*

Example: If you were pressured to take overtime in time, you would circle letter "D," and if in reaction you took the overtime in time <u>and</u> filed a grievance, you would write the numbers 4 and 6 after line D.

CONSEQUENCE YOU EXPERIENCED   **YOUR REACTION(S)**
(Circle one or more letter.)   *(Select one or more number from list below.)*

A. No consequences for making a lot of overtime .... ____ / ____ / ____ / ____
B. Had arrests reassigned to another officer. .... ____ / ____ / ____ / ____
C. Was admonished by ICO or other superior. .... ____ / ____ / ____ / ____
D. Was pressured to take overtime in compensation time
rather than cash .... ____ / ____ / ____ / ____
E. Was denied details or special assignments that offered
overtime. .... ____ / ____ / ____ / ____
F. Was given fewer patrol assignments with arrest opportunities. ____ / ____ / ____ / ____
G. Was threatened with reassignment / tour change /
RDO change. .... ____ / ____ / ____ / ____
H. Was reassigned or given tour change/RDO change. .... ____ / ____ / ____ / ____
I. Was threatened to not be able to work with steady partner. .. ____ / ____ / ____ / ____
J. Was forbidden to work with steady partner. .... ____ / ____ / ____ / ____
K. Was denied time off. .... ____ / ____ / ____ / ____
L. Was given lower evaluation. .... ____ / ____ / ____ / ____
M. Other_____ .... ____ / ____ / ____ / ____

POSSIBLE OFFICER REACTIONS
1. Did everything the same.
2. Made fewer arrests close to the end of tour.
3. Made fewer arrests generally.
4. Took overtime in comp time.
5. Tried to make <u>more</u> arrest overtime to make up for lost income.
6. Got PBA delegate involved / filed grievance.
7. Tried to get transfer to other unit.
8. Took second job / worked more at second job.
9. Other_____

72. In the past 12 months, about how many times, if at all, has a supervisor told you or hinted to you that you should be making more arrests? *(circle)*
Never   **1 time**   **2** times   **3** times   **4** times   **5** times   **6** times
7 times   **8** times   **9** times   **10** times   **12** times
(If you <u>never</u> were urged by a supervisor to make more arrests, write "N/A" over the rest of this page.)

73. The following is a list of consequences that police management may threaten, or actually impose, for not making enough arrests. Below and to the right is a list of ways officers may react to their bosses' actions.

In the first list, please indicate any consequence(s) <u>you</u> experienced. *(Circle the letter.)*

Then, from the list at the bottom, indicate <u>your</u> reaction(s) to each consequence you experienced. *(Write the number(s) of up to four different reactions for each consequence you circled in the blank lines that follow.)*

Example: If you were threatened with loss of permission to work a second job, you would circle letter "D," and if you reacted by making one arrest and "milking it" for overtime, you would write the numbers 2 and 4.

CONSEQUENCE YOU EXPERIENCED   YOUR REACTION
(Circle one or more letter:)   *(Select one or more number from list below.)*

A. No consequences threatened or imposed .... ____ / ____ / ___ _/ ____
B. Was given undesirable posts .... ____ / ____ / ____ / ____
C. Was told to take a specific arrest (e.g., shoplifter,
reassigned arrest) .... ____ / ____ / ____ / ____
D. Was threatened with loss of permission to work second job .. ____ / ____ / ____ / ____
E. Lost permission to work second job. .... ____ / ____ / ____ / ____
F. Was denied details or special assignments offering overtime . ____ / ____ / ____ / ____
G. Was given lower evaluation... ____ / ____ / ____ / ____
H. Was threatened with reassignment / tour change /
RDO change .... ____ / ____ / ____ / ____
I. Was reassigned / had tour changed / had RDO changed ...... ____ / ____ / ____ / ____
I. Was threatened to not be able to work with steady partner. ... ____ / ____ / ____ / ____
K. Was forbidden to work with steady partner .... ____ / ____ / ____ / ____
J. Was threatened with transfer. .... ____ / ____ / ____ / ___.
K. Was transferred.. ____ / ____ / ___ _/ ____
L. Was denied time off. .... ____ / ____ / ____ / ____
M. Other_____ ..... ____ / ____ / ____ / ____

POSSIBLE OFFICER REACTIONS
1. Did everything the same.
2. Made one routine arrest that month.
3. Made arrest for an offense that might otherwise get a summons.
4. Tried to "milk" the next arrest to make it worth the effort.
5. Made enough arrests to show "average" activity.
6. Tried to get steady "inside" assignment.
7. Got PBA delegate involved / filed grievance.
8. Other_____

Lastly, please complete the following demographic items, which are needed to analyze survey results:

74. Gender: **Male / Female**   *(Circle)*

75. Ethnic/Racial Affiliation *(Describe.)*_____

76. Age *(Write one number per line.)*   ___ ___

77. Highest Educational Level or Degree   *(Circle letter.)*
   A. H.S. Diploma
   B. Some college but no degree
   C. Associate degree
   D. B.A./B.S.
   E. Some graduate school but no degree
   F. M.A./M.S.
   G. J.D./Ph.D

78. Living with parents? **Yes / No**   *(Circle.)*

79. Living with spouse or "significant other"? **Yes / No**   *(Circle.)*

80. Living with children? **Yes / No**   *(Circle.)*

81. Ages of children (if any) living in your home *(Write one number per line.)*

___ ___ / ___ ___ / ___ ___ / ___ ___ / ___ ___ / ___ ___ / ___ ___ / ___ ___ / ___ ___ / ___ ___
 1st 2nd 3rd 4th 5th 6th 7th 8th 9th 10th
child   child   child   child   child   child   child   child   child   child

82. Living with dependent adult (elderly, ill, disabled, etc.) or child with exceptional
   needs? **Yes / No**   *(Circle)*
   Please explain circumstances _____

83. Living with another adult who shares in care-giving tasks (relative, home attendant,
   nanny etc.)? **Yes / No**   *(Circle)*
   Please explain circumstances _____

84. If there is other information about personal factors that you think is important in
   how you approach arrest-making, or if you want to clarify or comment on any aspect
   of the survey, please use the space below:

   _____
   _____
   _____
   _____
   _____
   _____

Survey of Police Agencies in Cities of Over 100,000 Population

JOHN JAY COLLEGE OF CRIMINAL JUSTICE

The City University of New York
899 Tenth Avenue, New York, N.Y. 10019
(212) 237-8000

June [ ], 2002

Chief of Police
[*City*] Police Department
[*Street Address*]
[*City, State, Zip Code*]

Dear Sir of Madam:

My name is Edith Linn and I am a lieutenant in the New York City Police Department. I am presently doing doctoral research, authorized by the NYPD and under a grant from the National Science Foundation, concerning how personal factors in police officers' lives affect their arrest decisions.

In the NYPD, the processing of an arrest involves a great deal of paperwork and close prisoner contact, and can take seven or more hours to complete. Thus when officers consider making arrests, they weigh such concerns as potential overtime, processing burdens, and disruption to their personal lives. I am interested in how other police departments process arrests, and whether they may have shorter or simpler procedures that exert less influence on the officers' arrest decisions. I would greatly appreciate your taking a few minutes to answer the following questions (continuing your response on the back of the page if space is insufficient):

1. About how long, on average, does it take an arresting officer from the time he or she makes an arrest to the time he or she resumes patrol or ends the tour? _____

_____

2. Are there other uniform or civilian members of your police agency that assist in processing an arrest, such as an arrest processing officer, fingerprint officer, cililian attendant, "paddy wagon" driver, or civilian clerical worker? Are there personnel from other agencies, such as correction officers, court officers, or members of the prosecutor's office, that assist in processing an arrest or handling the prisoner before arraignment? What are the titles, positions, and responsibilities of such individuals?

_____
_____
_____
_____
_____

3. What is the work schedule of the typical patrol officer? For instance, how long are the tours? How many days off are there between sets of tours? Do officers go around the clock or do they have steady tours? _____

_____

_____

4. Do arrests often cause officers to work past the end of their tours? Are they compensated in overtime time or money, and at what rate? Are they compensated or rewarded for making arrests in some other way? Please describe.

_____

_____

_____

5. What technology does your department use in processing arrests? For instance, do you electronically scan or send fingerprints and/or photos from one site to another? How are criminal histories (rap sheets) provided? Do arresting officers enter arrest information directly into a computer, without a hand-written first draft? Are arresting officers generally handy with computers, or do they rely on other designated individuals to enter data, etc? Do arresting officers have portable computers to use in processing arrest paperwork? Can your computer system transfer arrest information onto several different types of forms, or send arrest data to other units or outside agencies? Please describe.

_____

_____

_____

_____

_____

_____

6. Do you have any other information or suggestions that may help the NYPD to make arrest processing easier, quicker, or less of a factor in officers' arrest decisions? _____

_____

_____

Please use the enclosed self-addresses envelope to return your response. I also welcome further communication through mail (c/o Ph. D. program in Criminal Justice, 899 Tenth Avenue #433T, New York, NY 10019), e-mail (edie188@aol.com), or calls (718-438-8685). If I may contact a representative of your agency with further questions, please tell me how: _____

_____

Thank you very much for your help,

Edith Linn

61   See *Complaint Report.*

62A   Radio code: "Going into station house for administrative duties."

62P   Radio code: "Going into station house for 'personal necessity.'"

ADA   Assistant District Attorney.

Aided Card   A form prepared for an individual who is sick, injured, lost, emotionally disturbed, etc., and in need of assistance. Receives a serialized *Aided #.*

Arrest Report   A detailed form containing all information about an arrest. Receives a serialized *Arrest #.*

CCRB   Civilian Complaint Review Board: an independent mayoral agency, whose civilian members are empowered to investigate complaints against NYPD officers for excessive force, abuse of authority, discourtesy, or offensive language. The Board's findings, and in some instances, recommendations for discipline, are forwarded to the police commissioner.

CO   Commanding Officer.

Collar   Arrest.

Complaint Report The initial form (also called a **61**) prepared to report an unlawful act other situation requiring police investigation. Receives a serialized *Complaint #/ 61 #.*

COMPSTAT   Computer Comparison Statistics: a management approach that makes computerized data on crimes patterns and police performance promptly available to management. Precinct commanders are expected to rapidly respond to emerging problems and continuously assess their results. A key element is the weekly COMPSTAT meeting, wherein a panel of top police executives interrogate COs regarding negative developments in their precincts. Performance at COMPSTAT meetings is thought to be critical to a commanding officer's future career.

Comp time   Overtime compensation taken as time off from work, earned at time-and-a-half rates.

CONDOR   Citywide Organized Narcotics Drug Operational Response: a program begun in January 2000, in which officers on overtime tours make arrests for drugs and other specified offenses.

DAT   Desk Appearance Ticket: a notification to appear in court for arraignment at a future date. It is issued to persons arrested for misdemeanors and violations who meet other criteria (not intoxicated, no domestic offense involved, now outstanding warrants, etc.).

Dirtbag   A low-life, criminal.

DWI   Drinking while intoxicated.

EOT   End of tour.

IAB   Internal Affairs Bureau: A unit within the NYPD, reporting directly to the police commissioner, whose duties are to monitor the integrity of police officers and investigate allegations of corruption.

ICO   Integrity Control Officer: a supervisor, usually a lieutenant, whose integrity-monitoring duties include the investigation of excessive overtime.

IN-TAC   In-Service Tactics Training: a mandatory two-day course updating police tactics and other department matters, which every service member in the rank of police officer and detective attends once a year.

Jammed up   Accused of misconduct; facing departmental discipline

Livescan   Digital fingerprinting machine, which electronically captures and transmits prints

Looking   Shorthand for "looking for a collar"

MDT Mobile Digital Terminal: the computer mounted in patrol cars that allows officers to investigate a vehicle and its driver. MDT checks can reveal illegality before the driver is aware that he/she is being monitored. However, once the MDT check is performed, officers have no choice but to act on its information.

OLBS On-Line Booking System: the first computer system used by the NYPD to record and collects arrest report data. Replaced by the Omniform system in 2003.

OLPA On-line Prisoner Arraignment: a computer program that tracks prisoners from arrest to arraignment.

Omniform System A computer program introduced in 2003 for creating and storing Arrest Reports and Complaint Reports.

OT Overtime, most often referring to salary earned at time-and-a-half rates.

PAA Police Administrative Aide: a civilian clerical employee.

PBA Patrolmen's Benevolent Association: the police officers' union.

Perp Perpetrator of an offense.

Skell A derelict.

RDO Regular day(s) off.

Row Tow Rotation Tow: a protracted procedure for a found stolen vehicle, wherein the vehicle's contents are invoiced, a towing company under NYPD contract impounds the vehicle, and the owner is then notified.

Shitcan To discreetly dispose of an unwanted arrest or other messy situation.

UMOS Uniformed member of the service, i.e., police officer.

REFERENCES

Allport, G. W. (1933). *Institutional Behavior*. Chapel Hill: University of North Carolina Press.

Arcuri, A. F. (1977). Criminal justice: A police perspective. *Criminal Justice Review, 2*(1): 15–21.

Babbie, E. R. (2007). *The practice of social research* (11th ed.). Belmont, CA: Cengage.

Bahn, C. (1984). Police socialization in the eighties: Strains in the forging of an occupational identity. *Journal of Police Science and Administration* 12:390–394.

Baker, A. (2001, January 28). Sex and power vs. law and order. *New York Times*, pp. 21, 26.

Baker, A. (2002, February 23). Mayor says city can't afford higher raises for the police. *New York Times*, p. B1.

Banton, M. (1964) *The policeman in the community.* New York: Basic Books.

Barker, J. C. (1999). *Danger, duty, and disillusion: The worldview of Los Angeles police officers.* Prospect Heights, IL: Waveland Press.

Bailey, K. D. (1994). *Typologies and taxonomies: An introduction to classification techniques.* Sage University Paper Series on Quantitative Application in Social Sciences, 07. Thousand Oaks, CA: Sage.

Bayley, D. H. & Garofalo, J. (1989). The management of violence by police patrol officers. *Criminology, 27*, 1–25.

Bayley, D. H. & Worden, R. E. (1998). Police overtime: An examination of key issues. *National Institute of Justice Research in Brief.* Washington, D.C.: National Institute of Justice.

Becker, H. S. (1963). *Outsiders.* New York: Free Press.

Bell, D. J. (1985). Domestic violence: Victimization, police intervention, and disposition. *Journal of Criminal Justices, 13*, 525–534.

Bennett, W. W. & Hess, K. M. (2007). *Management and supervision in law enforcement.* Belmont, CA: Wadsworth/Thompson.

Berk, S. F. & Loseke, D. R. (1980). 'Handling' family violence: Situational determinants of police arrest in domestic disturbances. *Law and Society Review, 15*, 317–346.

Bittner, E. (1970). *The functions of the police in modern society.* Rockville, MD: Center for Studies of Crime and Delinquency, National Institute of Mental Health

Black, D. J. (1970). The production of crime rates. *American Sociological Review, 23*, 733–748.

Black, D. J. (1971). The social organization of arrest. *Stanford Law Review, 23*, 63–77.

Black, D. J. (1976) *The behavior of law.* New York: Academic Press.

Black, D. J. (1980). *The manners and customs of the police.* New York: Academic Press.

Black, D. J. & Reiss, A. J., Jr. (1967). *Studies of crime and law enforcement in metropolitan areas,* Vol. 2, Field Surveys III. Section 1: Patterns of behavior in police and citizen transactions. Washington, D.C.: Government Printing Office.

Black, D. J. & Reiss, A. J., Jr. (1970). Police control of juveniles. *American Sociological Review, 35,* 63–77.

Blumberg, A. (1997). The AIDS epidemic and the police. In R. G. Dunham & G.P. Alpert (Eds.), *Critical issues in policing* (3rd ed.). Prospect Heights, IL: Waveland Press.

Blumberg, A. S. & Niederhoffer, E. (Eds.) (1985). *The ambivalent force: Perspectives on the police* (3rd ed., pp. 214–224). New York: Holt, Rinehart & Winston.

Broderick, J. (1977). *Police in a time of change.* Morristown, NJ: General Learning Press.

Brooks, L. W. (1997). Police discretionary behavior: A study of style. In R. G. Dunham & G. P. Alpert (Eds.), *Critical issues in policing* (3rd ed., pp. 149–166). Prospect Heights, IL: Waveland Press.

Brown, M. K. (1988). *Working the street: Police discretion and the dilemmas of reform.* New York: Russell Sage Foundation.

Bumiller, E. (1999, November 20). In wake of attack, Giuliani cracks down on homeless. *New York Times,* p. A1.

Burbeck, E. & Furnham, A. (1985). Police officers selection: A critical view of the literature. *Journal of Police Science and Administration 13,* 58–69.

Caldwell, E. (1978). Patrol observation: The patrol encounter, patrol narrative, and general shift information forms. Police Services Study Methods Report MR-02. Bloomington, IN: Workshop in Political Theory and Policy Analysis.

Cardwell, D. (2001, January 12). Police demonstrate for a raise and denounce Giuliani. *New York Times,* p. B4.

Chappell, A. T., MacDonald, J. M., & Manz, P. W. (2006). The Organizational determinants of police arrest decisions. *Crime & Delinquency 52,* 287–306.

Chatterton, M. (1983). Police work and assault charges. In M. Punch (Ed.), *The police organization* (pp. 194–221). Cambridge: MIT Press.

Cochran, J. K. & Bromley, M. L. (2003). The myth (?) of the police subculture. *Policing 26,* 88–117.

Committee to Review Research on Police Policy and Practices. (2004). *Fairness and Effectiveness in Policing: The Evidence.* Washington, DC: National Academies Press.

Conlon, E. (2004). *Blue blood.* New York: Riverhead Books.

Cooper, M. & Lipton, E. (2002, January 4). City faces challenge to close widest budget gap. *New York Times,* p. A1.

Cooper, M. & Lipton, E. (2002, April 3). City's pension funds reel after taking a dual blow. *New York Times,* p. A1.

Coser, L. (1956). *The functions of social conflict.* Glencoe, IL: The Free Press.

Council for Community and Economic Research. (2002, Jan.) *ACCRA Cost of Living Index Publication for First Quarter, 2002.* Arlington, VA: ACCRA.

Crank, J. P. (1990). The influence of environmental & organizational factors on police style in urban & rural environments. *Journal of Research in Crime and Delinquency, 27,* 166–89.

Criminal Justice Bureau. (2001, December). *Arrest/arraignment indicators.* New York: New York City Police Department.

Criminal Justice Bureau. (2007, November). *Arrest/arraignment indicators.* New York: New York City Police Department.

Davis, K. C. (1969) *Discretionary justice: A preliminary inquiry.* Urbana: University of Illinois Press.

De La Cruz, D. (2000, May 3) Union ads: 'Don't join NYC police.' *Associated Press Online.* Retrieved May 7, 2008 from *http://library.kean.edu:2071/us/lnacademic/returnTodo?returnToKey=20_T369 7455129*

Dempsey, J. S. & Forst, L. S. (2005). *An introduction to policing* (4th ed.). Belmont, CA: Wadsworth Publishing Company.

Downs, A. (1967). *Inside bureaucracy.* Boston: Little, Brown.

Dworkin, R. (1977). *Taking rights seriously.* Cambridge: Harvard University Press.

Ericson, R.V. (1982). *Reproducing order: A study of police patrol work.* Toronto: University of Toronto Press.

Eterno, J. A. (2003). *Policing within the law.* Westport, CT: Praeger.

Eterno, J. A. & Silverman, E. B. (2006). The New York City Police Department's Compstat: Dream or Nightmare? *International Journal of Police Science and Management, 8(3),* 218–231.

Fayol, H. (1949). *General and industrial management.* London: Pittman.

Flynn, K. (2000, December 19). City hall and police union trade blame as talks stall. *New York Times,* p. B6.

Flynn, K. (2002, March 15). City's deficit forces police to study cuts in overtime. *New York Times,* p. B1.

Flynn, K. & Rashbaum, W. K. (2000, March 30). Some officers say Giuliani widens police-civilian gap. *New York Times,* p. A1.

Fogelson, R. (1977). *Big city police.* Cambridge: Harvard University Press.

Foley, M. O. (2000). *Police perjury: A factorial study.* Unpublished doctoral dissertation, City University of New York.

Forbell, M. P. (1973). *The commuting policeman: A comparison of the effectiveness of city and non-city resident New York City Police Department patrolmen.* Unpublished master's thesis, John Jay College of Criminal Justice, NY.

Geller, W. A. (1997). Suppose we were really serious about police departments becoming   learning organizations? *National Institute of Justice Journal, 234,* 2–8.

Goffman, E. (1959). *The presentation of self in everyday life.* Garden City, NY: Doubleday.

Goldstein, J. (1960). Police discretion not to invoke the criminal process: Low-visibility decisions in the administration of justice. *Yale Law Journal 69,* 543–588.

Greenhouse, S. (2000, July 29). Unions angered by city's proposal that police officers defer two weeks' pay. *New York Times,* p. B2.

Greenhouse, S. (2002, September 11). Arbitrator explains reasons behind police pay decision. *New York Times,* p. B5.

Guyot, D. (1991). *Policing as though people matter.* Philadelphia: Temple University Press.

Harrington, P. & Lonsway, K. A. (2004). Current barriers and future promise for women in policing. In B. F. Price & N. J. Sokoloff (Eds.), *The Criminal Justice System and Women* (3rd ed.) (pp. 495–510). New York: McGraw-Hill.

Herbert, S. (1998). Police subculture reconsidered. *Criminology, 36*: 343–368.

Hernandez, E. (1981). Influence of tight budgets on law enforcement. In J. Fyfe (Ed.), *Contemporary issues in law enforcement* (pp. 59–81). Beverly Hills, CA: Sage.

Herzberg, F. W. (1968, Jan.–Feb.). One more time: How do you motivate employees? *Harvard Business Review,* 54–62.

Holden, R. N. (1994). *Modern police management.* Englewood Cliffs, NJ: Prentice Hall.

Hollinger, R. C. (1984) Race, occupational status, and pro-active police arrest for drinking and driving. *Journal of Criminal Justice, 12,* 173–183.

Iannone, N. F. (1970). *Supervision of police personnel.* Englewood Cliffs, NJ: Prentice Hall.

Jermier, J. M., Slocum, J. L. Jr., Fry, L. W., & Gaines, J. (1991). Organizational subcultures in a soft bureaucracy: Resistance behind the myth and façade of an official culture. *Organization Science, 2,* 170–94.

Kahn, R. L., Wolfe, D. M., Quinn, R. P., & Snoek, J. D. (1964). *Organizational stress: Studies in role conflict and ambiguity.* New York: John Wiley & Sons.

Kappeler. V., Sluder, R., & Alpert, G. (1994). *Forces of Deviance: Understanding the Dark Side of Policing.* Prospect Heights: Waveland Press.

Karmen, A. (2003). *Crime victims: An introduction to victimology.* Belmont, CA: Wadsworth Publishing Company.

Katz, D. & Kahn, R. L. (1966). *The social psychology of organizations.* New York: John Wiley & Sons.

Kelling, G. & Sousa, W. H., Jr. (2001). *Do police matter? An analysis of New York City's police reforms.* (Civic Report 22). New York: Manhattan Institute for Policy Research.

Kerstetter, W. A. (1990). Gateway to justice: Police and prosecutorial response to sexual assaults against women. *Journal of Criminal Law, 82,* 267–313.

Kleinig, J. (Ed.) (1996). *Handled with discretion: Ethical issues in police decision making.* New York: Rowman & Littlefield Publishers, Inc.

Kleinig, J. (1997). *The ethics of policing.* Cambridge, U.K.: Cambridge University Press.

Klinger, D. A. (1994) Demeanor or crime? Why 'hostile' citizens are more likely to be arrested. *Criminology 32,* 631–656.

Klockars, C. (1983). *Thinking about the police: Contemporary readings.* New York: McGraw-Hill.

Krocs, W. (1985). *Society's victims—the police: An analysis of job stress in policing* (2nd ed.). Springfield, IL: Thomas.

Kroes, W. H., Margolis, B. L., & Hurrell, J. J. (1974). Job stress in policemen. *Journal of Police Science and Administration 2,* 145–155.

LaFave, W. (1965). *Arrest: The decision to take a suspect into custody.* Boston: Brown, Little.

Lafree, G. D. (1981). Official reactions to docial problems: Police decisions in sexual assault cases. *Social Problems, 28,* 582–594.

Lefkowitz, J. (1975). Psychological attributes of policemen: A review of research and opinion. *Journal of Social Issues 31,* 3–26.1

Lemert, E. M. (1967). *Human Deviance, Social Problems and Social Control.* Englewood Cliffs, NJ: Prentice Hall.

Leonard, V. A. & More, H. W. (1987). *Police organization and management* (7th ed.). Mineola, NY: The Foundation Press.

Liksa, A. E. & Chamlin, M. B. (1984). Social structure and crime control among macrosocial units. *American Journal of Sociology 90:* 383–395.

Linn, E. (2004). *What Works for Me? Arrest Decisions as Adaptive Behavior.* Ann Arbor, Michigan: University Microfilms International.

Lundman, R. J. (1974). Routine police arrest practices: A commonweal perspective. *Social Problems, 22,* 127–141.

Lundman, R. J. (1979). *Police and policing: An introduction.* New York: Holt, Rinehart, & Winston.

Lundman, R. J. (1980). Organizational norms and police discretion: An observational study of police work with traffic violators. *Criminology, 17,* 159–171.

Lundman, R. J., Sykes, R. E. & Clark, J. P. (1978). Police control of juveniles. *Journal of Research in Crime and Delinquency 15(1),* 74–91.

Manning, P. K. (1997). *Police work: The social organization of policing* (2nd ed.). Prospect Heights, IL: Waveland Press.

Martin, S. (1997). Women officers on the move: An update on women in policing. In R. G. Dunham & G. P. Alpert (Eds.), *Critical issues in policing* (3rd ed.). Prospect Hts., IL: Waveland Press.

Maslow, A. H. (1943). A theory of human motivation. *Psychological Review 50,* 370–396.

Mastrofski, S. D. (1981). Policing the beat: The impact of organizational scale on patrol officer behavior in urban residential neighborhoods. *Journal of Criminal Justice, 9,* 343–358.

Mastrofski, S. D. & Ritti, R. R.(1992). You can lead a horse to water... : A case study of a Police department's response to stricter drunk-driving laws. *Justice Quarterly, 9(3):* 465–491.

Mastrofski, S. D, Ritti, R. R., & Snipes, J. B. (1994). Expectancy theory and police productivity in DUI enforcement. *Law and Society Review, 28(1):* 113–148.

Mastrofski, S. D, Worden, R.E., & Snipes, J.B (1995). Law enforcement in a time of community policing. *Criminology. 33,* 539–564.

Mastrofski, S. D., Parks, R. B., Reiss, A. J., Worden, R. E., DeJong, C., Snipes, J. B., & Terrill, W. (1998). *Systematic Observation of Public Police.* Washington, DC: Government Printing Office.

Maynard, P. E. & Maynard, N. E. (1982). Stress in police families: Some policy implications. *Journal of Police Science and Administration, 10,* 302–314.

McCord, J., Wisdom, C. S., & Crowell, N. (Eds.) (2001). *Juvenile crime, juvenile justice.* Washington, DC: National Academy Press.

McDonald, B. (1999). *My father's gun: One family, three badges, one hundred years in the NYPD.* New York: Dutton.

McGregor, D. (1960). *The human side of enterprise.* New York: McGraw-Hill.

Merton, R. K. (1957). *Social theory and social structure.* New York: The Free Press.

More, H. W. & Wegener, W. F. (1992). *Behavioral police management.* New York: Macmillan.

Moyer, I. L. (1981). Demeanor, sex, and race in police processing. *Journal of Criminal Justice 9,* 235–246.

Muir, W. K. (1977). *Police: Streetcorner politicians.* Chicago: University of Chicago Press.

Munro, J. L. (1974). *Administrative behavior and police organization*. Cincinnati, OH: W.H. Anderson.

Narduli, P. (1978). *The courtroom elite: An organizational perspective on criminal justice*. Cambridge: Ballinger Publishing.

National Academy of Sciences. (2004). *Fairness and effectiveness in policing: The evidence*. Washington, DC: National Academy Press.

Niederhoffer, A. (1967). *Behind the shield: The police in urban society*. New York: Doubleday,

Novak, K. J., Frank, J., Smith, B. W.; & Engel, S. E. (2002). Revisiting the decision to arrest: Comparing beat and community officers. *Crime and Delinquency 48*, 70–98.

O'Neill, J. & Cushing, M. (1991). *The impact of shift work on police officers*. Washington, D.C.: Police Executive Research Forum.

Paoline, E. A. III, Myers, S. M., & Worden, R. E. (2000). Police culture, individualism, and community policing: Evidence from two police departments. *Justice Quarterly, 17*, 575–605.

Perrow, C. (1986). *Complex organizations: A critical essay*. New York: Random House.

Petersen, D. M. (1972). Police disposition of the petty offender. *Sociology and Social Research 56 (3)*, 320–330.

Piliavin, I. & Briar, S. (1964). Police encounters with juveniles. *American Journal of Sociology 70:* 206–14.

Rashbaum, W. K. (2008, January 23). Night shift has long ties to corruption. *The New York Times*, p. B4.

Reiss, A. J., Jr. (1971). *The police and the public*. New Haven, CT: Yale University Press.

Reuss-Ianni, E. (1983). The two cultures of policing: Street cops and management cops. *American Bar Foundation Research Journal, 1*, 206–213.

Rigoli, B., Crank, J. P., & Rivera, G. F. Jr. (1990). The construction and implementation of alternative measures of police cynicism. *Criminal Justice and Behavior, 17(4):* 395–409.

Riksheim, E. C. & Chermak, S. M. (1993). Causes of police behavior revisited. *Journal of Criminal Justice 21*, 352–382.

Roberg, R. R. & Kuykendall, J. (1997). *Police organization and management: Behavior, theory, process* (2nd ed.). Pacific Grove, CA: Brooks/Cole Publishing Company.

Roethlisberger, F. J. & Dickson, W. J. (1939). *Management and the worker*. Cambridge, MA: Harvard University Press.

Rosen, M. S. (1999). Interview with Prof. George Kelling. *Law Enforcement News, 25:* (511–512), 8–11+.

Rubinstein, J. (1973). *City police*. New York: John Wiley & Sons.

Selznick, P. (1948). Foundations of the theory of organization. *American Sociological Review 13*, 25–35.

Sharp, A. (1999). Off-duty employment. *Law & Order, 47(12),* 82–87.

Sherman, L. W. (1978). *Scandal and reform.* Los Angeles: University of California Press.

Sherman, L. W. (1980). Causes of police behavior: The current state of quantitative research. *Journal of Research in Crime and Delinquency, 17,* 69–100.

Sherman, L. W. (1990). Police crackdowns: Initial and residual deterrence. In M. Tonry & N. Morris (Eds.), *Crime and justice: A review of research.* Chicago: University of Chicago Press.

Sherman, L.W. (1992). *Policing domestic violence: Experiments and dilemmas.* New York: The Free Press.

Silverman, E. B. (1999). *NYPD battles crime.* Boston: Northeastern University Press.

Skolnick, J. H. (1966). *Justice without trial.* New York: John Wiley & Sons.

Skolnick, J. & Woodworth, J. R. (1967). Bureaucracy, information & social control. In D. Bordua (Ed.), *The police: Six sociological essays.* New York: John Wiley & Sons.

Smith, B. (1940). *Police systems in the United States.* New York: Harper.

Smith, D. A. (1982). *Invoking the law: Determinants of police arrest decisions.* Ann Arbor, Michigan: University Microfilms International.

Smith, D. A. (1984). The organizational aspects of legal control. *Criminology, 22:* 19–38.

Smith, D. A. (1986). The neighborhood context of police behavior. In A. J. Reiss, Jr. & M. Tonry (Eds.), *Communities and Crime* (pp. 313–341). Chicago: University of Chicago Press.

Smith, D. A. (1987). Police response to interpersonal violence: Defining the parameters of legal control. *Social Forces, 65,* 767–782.

Smith, D. A. & Klein, J. R. (1984). Police control of interpersonal disputes. *Social Problems, 31,* 468–481.

Smith, D. A. & Visher, C. A. (1981). Street level justice: Situational determinants of police arrest decisions. *Social Problems, 29:* 167–177.

Smith, D. A., Visher, C. A., & Davidson, L. A. (1984). Equity and discretionary justice: The influence of race on police arrest decisions. *Journal of Criminal Law, 75,* 234–249.

Sutherland, E. H. (1949). *White collar crime.* New York: Dryden Press.

Swanson, C. R., Territo, L., & Taylor, R. C. (1998). *Police administration: Structure, processes, and behavior.* Upper Saddle River, NJ: Prentice-Hall.

Sykes, R. E., Fox, J. C., & Clark, J. P. (1976) A socio-legal theory of police discretion. In A. Blumberg & E. Niederhoffer (Eds.), *The ambivalent force: Per-*

spectives on the police (3rd ed.) (pp. 171–183). New York: Holt, Rinehart & Winston.

Taylor, F. W. (1916). The principles of scientific management. *Bulletin of the Taylor Society.* Reprinted in J. Shafritz & J. A. Ott. (Eds.), *Classics of organizational theory* (1991). Pacific Grove, California: Brooks/Cole Publishing.

Territo, L. & Vetter, H. (1981). *Stress and police personnel.* Boston: Allyn & Bacon.

Turk, A. T. (1966). Conflict & criminality *American Sociological Review, 32,* 338–352.

Van Maanen, J. (1975). Police socialization: A longitudinal examination of job attitudes in an urban police department. *Administrative Science Quarterly, 20,* 207–228.

Van Maanen, J. (1983). The boss: First line supervision in an American police agency. In M. Punch (Ed.), *Control in the police organization.* Cambridge, MA: MIT Press.

Van Maanen, J. & Manning, P. K. (1978). *Policing: A view from the street.* New York: Random House.

Vila, B. & Taiji, E. Y. (1999) Police work hours, fatigue, and officer performance. In Kenney, D. J., & McNamara, R. P. (Eds.), *Police and policing: Contemporary issues.* Westport, CT: Praeger.

Vingilis, E., Blefgen, H., Colbourne, D., Reynolds, D., Waslyk, N., & Solomon, R. (1986). Police enforcement practices and perceptions of drinking-driving laws. *Canadian Journal of Criminology, 28,* 147.

Violanti, J. M. & Aron, F. (1995). Police stressors: variations in perception among police personnel. *Journal of Criminal Justice, 23,* 287–294.

Visher, C. A. (1983). Gender, police arrest decisions, and notions of chivalry. *Criminology, 21,* 5–28.

Vold, G. B. (1979). *Theoretical criminology* (2nd ed.). New York: Oxford University Press.

Vollmer, A. (1936). *The police and modern society.* Berkeley, CA: University of California Press. Reprinted Patterson (1971).

Vroom, V. H. (1964). *Work and motivation.* New York: John Wiley & Sons.

Walker, S. (1993) *Taming the system: The control of discretion in criminal justice 1950–1990.* New York: Oxford Press, 1993.

Walker, S. & Katz, C. M. (2008). *The police in America: An introduction* (6th ed.) New York: McGraw-Hill.

Walsh, W. F. (1986). Patrol officer arrest rates: A study of the social organization of police work. *Justice Quarterly, 3,* 271–290.

White, M. D. (2007). *Current issues and controversies in policing.* Boston: Allyn and Bacon.

Weber, M. (1946). *From Max Weber: Essays in sociology.* Edited & translated by H.
    H. Gerth & C. W. Mills. New York: Oxford University Press.

Weisburg, D., Mastrofski, S. D., McNally, A. M., Greenspan, R., & Willis, J. J.
    (2003). Reforming to preserve: Compstat and strategic problem-solving in
    American policing. *Criminology and Public Policy, 3:* 421–455.

Weiss, M. (2001, January 10). PBA to stage rally in bid to prod mayor. *The New
    York Post,* p. 27.

Westley, W. (1970). *Violence and the police.* Cambridge: MIT Press.

Whisenand, P. M. (1981). *The effective police manager.* Englewood Cliffs: Pren-
    tice-Hall.

White, S. (1972). A perspective on police professionalization. *Law and Society
    Review, 7,* 61–85.

Wilson, J. Q. (1968). *Varieties of police behavior: The management of law in eight
    communities.* Cambridge, MA: Harvard University Press.

Wilson, J. Q. (1974). Crime and the criminologists. *Commentary,* 58, 47–53.

Wilson, J. Q. (1989*). Bureaucracy: What government agencies do and why they do it.*
    New York: Basic Books.

Wilson, J. Q. & Kelling, G. (1982, March). Broken windows: The police and
    neighborhood safety. *Atlantic Monthly* 249. 29–39.

Wilson, O. W. (1950). *Police administration.* New York: McGraw-Hill.

Worden, R. E. (1989). Situational and attitudinal explanations of police be-
    havior: A theoretical appraisal and empirical assessment. *Law and Society
    Review, 23,* 667–711.

Worden, R. E. (1995). Police Officer's Belief Systems: A framework for analy-
    sis. *American Journal of Police, 14,* 49–81.

Worden, R. E. & Politz, A. A. (1984). Police arrests in domestic disturbances:
    A further look. *Law and Society Review, 18,* 105–119.

INDEX

Note: Page locators followed by f or t refer to figures and tables.

NEW PERSPECTIVES
IN CRIMINOLOGY
AND CRIMINAL JUSTICE

Jeffrey Ian Ross, *General Editor*

This book series is a forum for cutting-edge work that pushes the boundaries of the disciplines of criminology and criminal justice, with the aim of exploring eclectic, un- and under-explored issues, and imaginative approaches in terms of theory and methods. Although primarily designed for criminology and criminal justice audiences—including scholars, instructors, and students—books in the series function across disciplines, appealing to those with an interest in anthropology, cultural studies, sociology, political science, and law.

Books in the series include:

Hawking Hits on the Information Highway, by Laura Finley
Blood, Power and Bedlam: State Crimes and Crimes Against Humanity in Post-Colonial Africa, by Christopher W. Mullins and Dawn L. Rothe
Chinese Policing: History and Reform, by Kam C. Wong
Arrest Decisions: What Works for the Officer? by Edith Linn
Drug Court Justice: Experiences in a Juvenile Drug Court, by Kevin Whiteacre

Authors who would like to submit a proposal for a volume in the series, or a completed book manuscript please direct all inquiries to:

Chris Myers, Peter Lang Publishing, 29 Broadway, New York, NY, 10006
ChrisM@plang.com

To order other books in this series, please contact our Customer Service Department:

800-770-LANG (within the U.S.)
212-647-7706 (outside the U.S.)
212-647-7707 FAX

Or browse online by series at:
www.peterlang.com